To Our Readers

Every day, there are times when you want to know more about something. It may be about how plants grow, or how electric motors work. You may want a certain fact about Abraham Lincoln, earth satellites, Bolivia, the invention of the piano, or what causes colds —to take just a few examples. Sometimes you need more information than a teacher, your parents, or a schoolbook can give. That's the time to turn to your GOLDEN BOOK ENCYCLOPEDIA.

This encyclopedia *is* for you. It has been made especially for readers who are starting to look up information on their own, and who want that information on their own bookshelf.

Into this encyclopedia have been put the most important facts of modern knowledge. The thousands of articles and color pictures, charts, diagrams, and maps make all this knowledge clear and exciting. Here is an endless parade of fascinating facts—facts you can depend upon for up-to-dateness and accuracy, because world-famous experts have checked them. Get into the habit of looking things up in your GOLDEN BOOK ENCYCLOPEDIA. Use it to discover more about interesting subjects mentioned in school. Let it be your partner in homework and school projects.

Watch newspapers and television for important news about science and government, foreign countries, famous people, sports, plants and animals, literature and art, weather and exploration. Look up these subjects in the index of your GOLDEN BOOK ENCYCLOPEDIA. Then read about them.

In the evening, or on a rainy day, pick up any volume of your GOLDEN BOOK ENCYCLOPEDIA. Open it anywhere and start reading. Notice how interesting just about any subject can be when it is clearly explained and well pictured. You will find yourself getting interested in more and more kinds of information.

THE GOLDEN BOOK ENCYCLOPEDIA is your guide to knowledge. The more you read it, the better you will like it.

THE EDITORS

THE
GOLDEN BOOK
ENCYCLOPEDIA

VOLUME III—BOATS TO CEREALS

In Sixteen Accurate, Fact-filled Volumes Dramatically Illustrated
with More Than 6,000 Color Pictures

THE ONLY ENCYCLOPEDIA FOR YOUNG GRADE-SCHOOL CHILDREN

ACCURATE AND AUTHORITATIVE

ENTERTAININGLY WRITTEN AND ILLUSTRATED TO
MAKE LEARNING AN ADVENTURE

by Bertha Morris Parker

*Formerly of the Laboratory Schools, University of Chicago
Research Associate, Chicago Natural History Museum*

GOLDEN PRESS · NEW YORK

CONTRIBUTORS AND CONSULTANTS

HALL BARTLETT, *Ed.D., Citizenship Education Project, Teachers College, Columbia University; Author*

WALT DISNEY, *Motion Picture and Television Producer*

EVELYN MILLIS DUVALL, *Ph.D., Author and Consultant on Family Life; Authority on Child Development*

EDNA E. EISEN, *Ph.D., Professor of Geography, Kent State University*

J. ALLEN HYNEK, *Ph.D., Associate Director, Smithsonian Astrophysical Observatory*

LELAND B. JACOBS, *Ph.D., Professor of Education, Teachers College, Columbia University*

ELEANOR M. JOHNSON, *M.A., Director of Elementary School Services, Graduate Division, Wesleyan University*

HERBERT A. LANDRY, *M.S., Ph.D., Director, Bureau of Educational Program Research and Statistics, New York City Public Schools*

MILTON LEVINE, *M.D., Associate Professor of Pediatrics, New York Hospital*

WILLY LEY, *Professor of Science, Fairleigh Dickinson University; Rocket Expert and Author*

NORMAN LLOYD, *M.A., Teacher of Literature and Materials of Music, Juilliard School of Music*

LENOX R. LOHR, *M.E., D.Eng., D.Sc., President, Museum of Science and Industry, Chicago*

WILL C. MCKERN, *D.S., Former Director, Milwaukee Public Museum; Anthropologist*

RICHARD A. MARTIN, *B.S., Curator, N. W. Harris Public School Extension, Chicago Natural History Museum*

MAURICE PATE, *Executive Director, United Nations Children's Fund (UNICEF)*

NORMAN VINCENT PEALE, *D.D., LL.D., Litt.D., LH.D.; Minister, Marble Collegiate Church, New York; Author*

RUTHERFORD PLATT, *B.A., Member of Two North Pole Expeditions with Admiral MacMillan; Author of Nature Books*

ILLA PODENDORF, *M.S., Teacher of Science, University of Chicago Laboratory Schools; Author of Science Books*

MARY M. REED, *Ph.D., Supervisor of Little Golden Books; Formerly of Teachers College, Columbia University*

JOHN R. SAUNDERS, *M.A., Chairman, Department of Public Instruction, American Museum of Natural History*

GLENN T. SEABORG, *Ph.D., LL.D., D.Sc., Chancellor and Professor of Chemistry, University of California, Berkeley; Associate Director, University of California Radiation Laboratory; Co-winner of Nobel Prize for Chemistry, 1951*

LOUIS SHORES, *Ph.D., Dean of the Library School, Florida State University; Author and Authority on Reference Materials*

NILA BANTON SMITH, *Ph.B., Ph.D., Professor of Education and Director of The Reading Institute, New York University*

BRYAN SWAN, *M.S., Teacher of Physical Science, University of Chicago Laboratory Schools; Author*

SAMUEL TERRIEN, *S.T.M., Th.D., Auburn Professor of the Old Testament, Union Theological Seminary*

JESSIE TODD, *M.A., Formerly of the Art Department, University of Chicago; Art Lecturer; Contributor to Art Magazines*

LLOYD B. URDAL, *Ph.D., Assistant Professor, School of Education, State College of Washington*

JANE WERNER WATSON, *B.A., Editor and Author of More Than a Hundred Golden Books*

WILLIAM S. WEICHERT, *M.S., Supervisor of Science, Oakland (Calif.) Public Schools*

PAUL A. WITTY, *Ph.D., Professor of Education, Northwestern University; Specialist on Gifted Children*

STAFF

ROBERT D. BEZUCHA, *Project Director;* NORMAN F. GUESS, *Editorial Director;* R. JAMES ERTEL, *Managing Editor;* PAULINE NORTON, *Assistant Project Director;* ALICE F. MARTIN, *Associate Editor. Staff Editors:* GENEVIEVE CURLEY, JOAN FALK, HESTER GELB, RICHARD D. HARKINS.

The first boat was a log. Then men learned to make rafts and dugouts from logs.

BOATS Oceans and rivers are now highways. But in the days of our earliest ancestors they were not. A land separated from another by an ocean was as unreachable as if it had been on another planet. And before man learned to make boats, wide rivers were like high fences separating the land on the two banks. Boats gave early man a way of traveling on water. Later they came to be very important in the spread of civilization.

Some early man may have got the idea of a boat in this way: Standing on the edge of a river, he saw signs of good hunting on the other side. A log from a dead tree floated by. Perhaps, he thought, he could ride on the log. Perhaps if he kicked his feet he could steer the log across the river. He tried out his idea and it worked.

We can at least be fairly sure that men learned to ride on logs before they built anything for traveling on water. Once people had the idea of riding on logs it was an easy step to tie several logs together with vines or strips of skin. In this way rafts began. It must have been an easy step, too,

to hollow out a log and ride in it instead of on it. No one knows where such a boat was first made or who made it.

Even today there are boats that are just hollowed-out logs. They are called dugouts.

People often wanted boats in places where they could not get logs. They learned to make them of other things. Skin and reeds are two materials that many different peoples used. A boat made of skin or reeds has to be coated with something that will make it waterproof.

At the same time that our early ancestors were learning how to make boats, they were discovering ways of pushing them along. They found out that they could push them with poles or oars or paddles. They learned how to make the wind help them. They invented sails.

When we say that anything is boat-shaped, we mean that it is shaped like this: ◁▷ But many boats are not this shape at all. Some are pointed at one end and flat at the other. Some are round.

On our rivers and lakes and seas today there are swarms of boats. Some of them

Men discovered how to use sails for speed, and how to use reeds and skins in building boats.

Canalboats were towed upstream.

Rowboats are both useful and fun.

Schooners are now pleasure craft.

are used just for fun. But many of them are very useful ways of traveling. Some boats of today are even the homes of the people who own them. We call these house-boats. We still have boats with paddles and boats with oars and boats with sails. And now we have boats with motors, too.

After men had learned to make small boats, they learned to make big boats, or ships. But the story of ships is another story. (See HOUSEBOATS; SHIPS.)

TYPES OF SAILING VESSELS

Bark

Barkentine

Brigantine

Brig

Schooner

Sloop

Whaleboats are no match for an angry whale.

Motorboating has become a popular sport.

BODY, HUMAN What are boys and girls made of? There is a Mother Goose rhyme that gives an answer to this question. But of course the answer is wrong. Girls are not made of "sugar and spice and all things nice," and boys are not made of "snips and snails and puppy dog tails." The list below gives the *right* answer. The answer is the same for both boys and girls. It is the same for grown people, too.

Calcium	Hydrogen	Oxygen
Carbon	Iodine	Potassium
Chlorine	Iron	Phosphorus
Cobalt	Magnesium	Sodium
Copper	Manganese	Sulfur
Fluorine	Nitrogen	Zinc

These names are the names of elements. Our bodies are made of elements just as everything else in the world is.

But knowing what elements are in our bodies is only a tiny start in knowing how we are built. Knowing that a big steam engine is made mostly of iron does not help us know about its parts and how it works.

Our bodies are wonderful machines. They are far more wonderful than any machines that men have ever built. Like all living things, they are made of tiny blocks of living material called cells. The cells are made of protoplasm. Protoplasm is a mysterious substance. Scientists know what elements it has in it, but they cannot put these elements together to make it.

There are billions of cells in a person's body. They are so tiny that no one can see them without a microscope. The cells are not all alike. There are many different

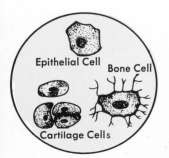

Epithelial Cell
Bone Cell
Cartilage Cells
Nerve Cell
Muscle Cell
Fat Tissue

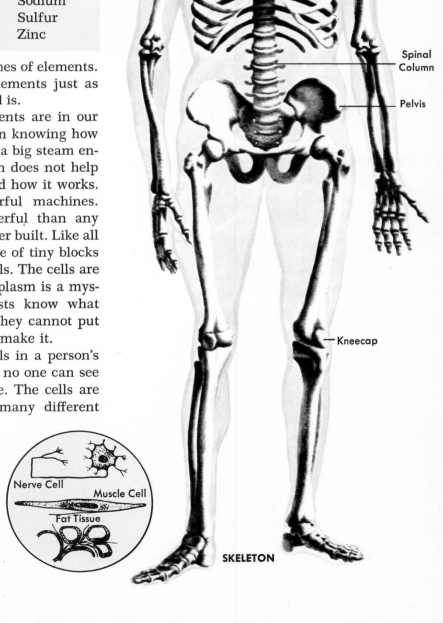

Skull
Collarbone
Shoulder Blade
Breastbone
Ribs
Spinal Column
Pelvis
Kneecap

SKELETON

kinds. Our muscles are very different from our bones because they are made of different kinds of cells. Our brains are not at all like our stomachs because the cells in them are not alike. Some parts of our bodies are made of cells of several different kinds.

The following pictures tell a little bit of the story of how our bodies are built.

Our bones make a framework for our bodies. They give us our shape. They protect the inner parts of our bodies, too.

Fastened to the bones are the muscles that let us move about. We would be as helpless as wooden dolls if it were not for

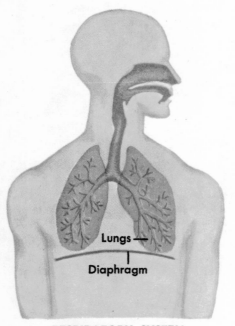

RESPIRATORY SYSTEM

these muscles. We also have some muscles that are not fastened to bones. The heart and the stomach are made of muscle.

The heart is a pump that keeps blood flowing through our bodies. The blood carries food and water and oxygen to all parts of our bodies. Then it carries waste materials away. Blood is so important that the heart has to keep pumping it every minute of every day of our lives. The blood travels through blood vessels of three kinds: veins, arteries, and capillaries. Arteries carry the blood away from the heart. Veins bring it

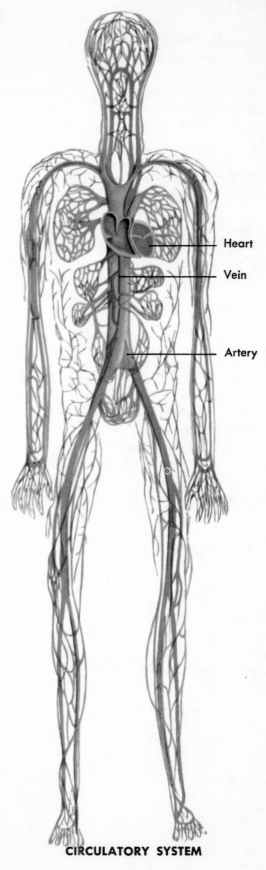

CIRCULATORY SYSTEM

back to the heart. Capillaries join the veins to the arteries.

Our bodies have air pumps, too. The air pumps are the lungs. The lungs are masses of tubes and tiny sacs. Air comes into them through the nose, throat, windpipe, and the

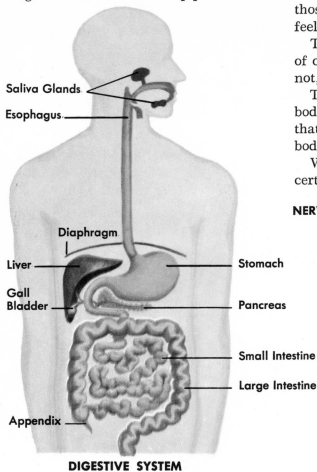

Saliva Glands

Esophagus

Diaphragm

Liver

Stomach

Gall Bladder

Pancreas

Small Intestine

Large Intestine

Appendix

DIGESTIVE SYSTEM

bronchial tubes. Really the lungs themselves do not do the pumping. The pumping is done by a thick wall of muscle called the diaphragm and by the ribs.

As the body works, it produces waste materials. The blood gathers up this waste, but there must be a way of getting rid of it. The kidneys do most of this work.

Everyone knows that our bodies have to have food. But they cannot use food until it has been digested. Digesting food is not simple. Many parts of our bodies are needed for changing food so that it can be used.

Our bodies could not do their work if it were not for our nervous systems. Our nervous systems are made up of our brain, our spinal cord, and our nerves. The nerves are the telegraph lines of our bodies. Among the messages that travel over our nerves are those that let us see, hear, taste, smell, and feel.

The pictures do not show all the parts of our wonderful body machines. They do not, for instance, show the glands.

There are glands of different kinds in our bodies. These glands produce chemicals that are very important in making our bodies work as they should.

We would be very queer looking and certainly not very handsome if the inside

NERVOUS SYSTEM

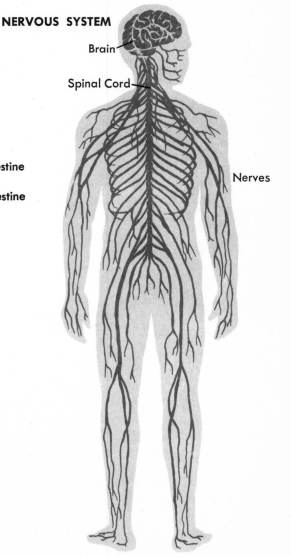

Brain

Spinal Cord

Nerves

parts of our bodies showed. The skin makes a good covering. It also helps keep our bodies the right temperature. And it gets rid of some waste. The skin has many different kinds of cells in it.

No man-made machine has any parts as wonderful as our eyes or our hearts or our brains. There are other ways in which our bodies are far ahead of any man-made machine: They can grow. They can mend themselves if they are injured. And they can have babies. Think of a big locomotive that could mend its smokestack if it were broken, and could grow to be 20 times as big as it was when it was made, and could produce new little locomotives!

Every human being begins life as a single cell. But it is a very special kind of

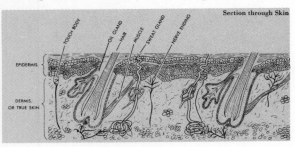
Section through Skin

TOUCH BODY · OR GLAND · HAIR · MUSCLE · SWEAT GLAND · NERVE ENDING

EPIDERMIS

DERMIS OR TRUE SKIN

cell. It is made by the union of two other cells. One of these is called a sperm. It is made in a male organ called a testis. The other is called an egg. It is made in a female organ called an ovary. The sperm and the egg have to meet and join before a baby can be born. The joining comes about when the mother and father mate. The sperm enters the mother's body and unites with the egg. The egg then starts to grow. After a while it enters another organ in the mother's body called the uterus. It is here that the baby grows until it is ready to be born.

A new life starts when a baby is born.

BOLÍVAR, SIMÓN (1783-1830) Every land has its heroes. Simón Bolívar is one of the great heroes of South America.

Simón Bolívar was born in Venezuela. At that time Venezuela was a part of a big Spanish colony ruled by Spain. Bolívar's family was rich and important. When he was 19 he was sent to Spain to be educated. There he married a beautiful Spanish girl. He took her back to Venezuela, but she died a few months later. Bolívar was heartbroken. He went once again to Europe.

In Europe Bolívar met some South Americans who were trying to get help in freeing their lands from Spain. Bolívar saw then how he could make his life worth living—he would fight for freedom.

He and the men who joined him had many defeats and discouragements. But at last they succeeded in freeing the lands which are now Venezuela, Colombia, and Ecuador. Bolívar became the president of the three together. Then he helped free Peru. Part of Peru became Bolivia—named in Bolívar's honor.

Freedom from Spain did not bring peace to these countries that were freed. Bolívar had to rush from one place to another to handle outbreaks of fighting. Some of his earlier friends became enemies. At last he refused to lead the new nations any longer. Soon afterward he died.

Just before Bolívar died, he said that he had "plowed the sea." He meant that what he had done was as useless as making a furrow on the surface of the ocean. But the people of South America came to realize that he was a really great leader.

BOLIVIA Two countries in South America have no seacoast. Bolivia is one of them. This country lies partly on a high plateau in the Andes Mountains. But more than half its area is lowland.

Bolivia is over seven times as big as Illinois. But it has less than half as many people. Most of them are either pure Indian, or part Indian and part Spanish.

Some of the lowland is grassland. Some is dense forest. Heat and moisture make the climate almost unbearable. Few people live there.

Many more live on the eastern slopes of the Andes. Here the climate is pleasanter, and the soil is rich. But the people are very much shut off from the rest of the world by the peaks of the Andes. Getting what they raise to market means carrying it up steep mountain slopes.

More than half the people of Bolivia live on the plateau. But here life is not easy either. The plateau is so high that the nights are always cold. It is so dry that there are no trees. Fuel is scarce. Only a few kinds of crops can be raised.

Many of the people barely make a living. Some are farmers. Some gather salt. Some fish in Lake Titicaca, the biggest freshwater lake in South America. Others drive caravans of llamas. Still others are miners.

Bolivia would be poor indeed if it were not for its mines. Once the country was famous for its gold and silver. Now it is more famous for its tin. It also has copper and lead. But even mining is harder here than in most places. Some of the mines are more than three miles above sea level. Many workmen cannot do heavy work in the thin air of such heights.

La Paz, Bolivia's capital, is the highest capital in the world. The city lies in a valley in the plateau. On market days Indians in bright-colored shawls or ponchos come down steep trails to the city with things to sell. They bring big loads on their backs or on the backs of llamas and donkeys. They may have woolen cloth they have woven, or peppers or potatoes they have raised. They may have coca leaves, which Bolivians like to chew, or tropical fruits. They spread out their wares along the curbs. La Paz becomes a colorful spot in the bleak plateau. (See ANDES.)

Indians use llamas to bring their goods into La Paz on market day.

A Woman of Bombay

BOMBAY The city of Bombay has become the largest city of crowded India. In just the past few years it has gone ahead of Calcutta. Today Bombay is one of the largest cities of the world.

Bombay is on an island close to the west coast of the peninsula of India. It is on an excellent harbor. From all over the world ships come to its wharves. The city serves as the chief gateway to western India. Railroads leading from it carry far and wide the goods unloaded from the ships.

The building of the Suez Canal nearly a hundred years ago started Bombay on its way to becoming a great city. Ships coming through the canal could reach it easily. Mills for weaving cloth from the cotton raised in India sprang up in Bombay. From there the cloth could be shipped to all parts of the world. Today the city leads India in the weaving of cotton.

The business section of Bombay looks much like the business section of an American city. There are many modern buildings. But, like Calcutta, it also has ugly slums. In the older parts of the city there are many narrow unpaved streets along which sacred cows still wander. (See CALCUTTA; INDIA.)

BONES Clams and bees and jellyfish do not have bones. Neither do thousands of other animals. The only animals that do are fishes, amphibians, reptiles, birds, and mammals. They have bony skeletons.

Bone is made of cells, just as other living tissues are. As bones grow, new bone cells are made and old ones are destroyed.

Some "bone" is not true bone. Cuttlebone, for instance, is not. It comes from the cuttlefish, which is really not a fish. Names do not always tell a true story. (See BODY, HUMAN; SKELETON.)

BOOKS AND BOOKBINDING Books today are so easy to get that it is hard to think of a time when there were no books. But for thousands and thousands of years there were no books at all. In very early times there could not be any books, because people did not know how to write. Even after men learned to write, it was a long time before they made books.

The first books, as far as anyone knows, were made in Egypt more than 5,000 years ago. These first books were made of papyrus. Papyrus was somewhat like paper, but it was more brittle. It was made from the stems of a water plant that grew along the Nile River.

Some ancient roll books were 144 feet long.

The first books were not made of pages bound together inside a cover. Instead, sheets, or pages, of papyrus were pasted together to form a long strip. A strip might be as long as 144 feet. One end of each strip was fastened to a small rod of wood or bone. Usually the other end was fastened to a rod, too. The whole strip was rolled up around one rod. A roll book was a little like a window shade.

It took two hands to read a roll book. The reader rolled up the part he had read with one hand while he unrolled new pages with the other. A book was kept closed with strings or straps. Often roll books were carried from place to place in boxes shaped like round hatboxes.

The first books made of pages bound together in a cover were made of parchment. Parchment was made from animal skins. Vellum, one kind of parchment, came from the skins of young lambs or calves or kids. Frequently it was no thicker than ordinary paper is now.

Of course, all the books of ancient times, whether they were made of papyrus or parchment, were written by hand. The only way to make a copy of a book was to copy it by hand. In Roman times slaves did most of this copying.

During the Middle Ages most of the copying of books was done by monks. It often took months, sometimes years, of hard work for the monks to copy a single book by hand. Besides, they often decorated the pages of the books they copied. As a rule, beginning letters were beautifully colored. Sometimes they were made of thin sheets of pure gold.

Books could never be cheap and plentiful so long as parchment had to be used for their pages and so long as they had to be written by hand. But two inventions made the story very different. Paper and printing were invented. Paper was very much cheaper than parchment, and printing made it possible to have as many copies of a book as were wanted.

Monks copied books by hand.

At first people made fun of printed books. A great book collector who lived 500 years ago boasted that every book he had was "written with the pen." He said that he would be ashamed to put a printed book in his library. But printed books soon won their way and printing shops sprang up all over Europe.

All the books that were printed when printing was in its babyhood—from the year 1455 to 1500—are called "cradle books." Some of the cradle books are among the most beautiful books ever made. Often they were decorated by hand after they were printed.

Probably the most famous of all the cradle books are the Gutenberg Bibles. Gutenberg is often called the inventor of printing with movable type. For a long time people thought the Gutenberg Bible was printed by Gutenberg. But very likely a printer named Schoeffer printed it. How surprised Schoeffer would have been if he had known that copies of this book would someday be worth their weight in gold. Not many years ago $500,000 was paid for a single copy.

The first book ever printed in English came from the press of the English printer William Caxton in 1474. The book was about the ancient city of Troy.

If Gutenberg and Schoeffer and Caxton could wander into one of our great book-making establishments of today, they

would certainly be amazed at the changes that have taken place in bookmaking. Modern books like this one go through a series of steps in which most of the work is done by machine. These different steps include printing, folding, gluing, sewing, and fitting with covers.

Books of today are not printed page by page, as old books were. Instead, a great many pages are printed at one time on a large sheet of paper. The sheet is then folded over and over so that it makes a bundle of pages. After the folding, the pages are all in the right order. These bundles of pages are called "signatures."

After the printing and folding are done, all the signatures that make up a book are gathered together. Books that have many signatures will be thick. Books with only a few will be thin. In many books the signatures are then sewed together on special machines. There are several different methods of sewing. Many thick books have holes drilled in them for the thread to go through. Others are sewed on machines that work like home sewing machines. When the sewing is completed, the pages of the book are trimmed to the correct size.

The next step is to get the book ready for its "case," which is the name bookbind-ers give to the cover of a book. Special machines make the back of the book round and also glue on a strip of gauze material called "super."

The covers of the book are made separately. If the book is to be bound in cloth covers, the cloth is first cut from a roll into sections that will fit the book. The cloth is then glued onto special "boards," which are actually a form of thick, stiff cardboard.

After work is finished on the book and on the covers, the two are brought together. A machine puts paste on the end papers of the book and puts it into the case. Men inspect the book carefully to see that it fits perfectly in its case and that none of the pages are upside down. If the book passes inspection, it is ready to be packaged and shipped out.

Most of the work which is now done by machine had to be done by hand in the days of Gutenberg and Schoeffer and Caxton. The giant modern press that printed this book even printed the colored pictures along with the type. Gutenberg and Schoeffer and Caxton would have had to color them by hand. Books have come a long way from the papyrus roll books of the ancient Egyptians. (See COPYRIGHT; PAPER; PAPYRUS; PRINTING; WRITING.)

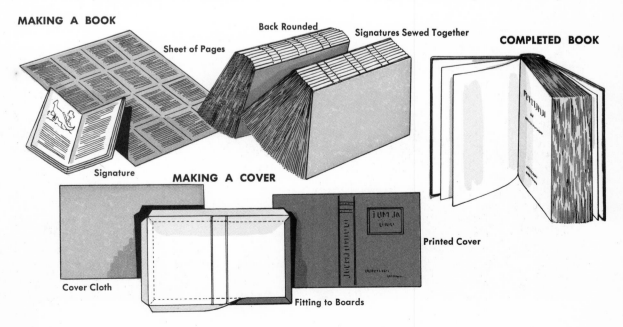

MAKING A BOOK

Sheet of Pages

Back Rounded

Signatures Sewed Together

COMPLETED BOOK

Signature

MAKING A COVER

Cover Cloth

Fitting to Boards

Printed Cover

BOOMERANG The man in the picture is an Australian native. The club he is about to throw is a boomerang. When thrown, the boomerang will first fly forward, spinning as it goes. Then it will turn around in the air and come back to the thrower.

A skillful thrower can make his boomerang do many stunts. He can make it bounce off the ground several times before it rises into the air and starts back. He can make it loop-the-loop several times. He can even make it turn in a figure-eight in the air.

A boomerang is simply a curved club. But it must be curved in exactly the right way. It must be curved so that the air pushing against it will make it do its stunts. Some boomerangs are carved from small trees which already have a good bend. It may be at a place where a branch joins the trunk. Some boomerangs are made from straight pieces of wood that are first soaked in water and then bent into shape.

There are also boomerangs that do not return to the thrower. These are rather heavy and are almost straight. They make better weapons, but they are not as interesting to watch.

The boomerang is a strange, but effective, weapon.

Daniel was captured by Indians several times.

BOONE, DANIEL (1734-1820) Of all the early American pioneers, Daniel Boone is the most famous. The trails he blazed helped open up the great stretch of land beyond the Appalachians.

In colonial days, when Daniel was a boy, much of America was still a wilderness. Even the region in Pennsylvania where he was born was rather wild. Indians roamed the forests near by. There were bears and other wild animals in the forests, too. Daniel was given a rifle when he was 12 years old. He often went into the woods to hunt. He learned to know every trail through the forests. He was friendly with the Indians and learned many of their ways.

Later Daniel moved with his family to North Carolina. His home there was also on the edge of the wilderness.

When Daniel was a young man he became a soldier. He fought with the English in a war against the Indians. During that war he heard of the beautiful country west of the mountains. Not long afterward he and a few companions crossed the Blue Ridge Mountains through Cumberland Gap and went on into what is now Kentucky. He was gone for two years.

In 1769, with the help of 30 men, Boone cut the famous 300-mile Wilderness Road that led to the Kentucky River. At the end of this long trail Boone founded the town of Boonesborough.

Boone's wife and daughter were the first

white women to come to this part of the country. Daniel thought the wild new land was a paradise. He told other families about the great supply of game there. He told them of the big rivers and rich forests. He urged them to come to this new country to settle with their families. In 1775 he led the first group of settlers over the mountains into Kentucky, along the trails he had blazed earlier.

Later he moved with his family to Missouri and journeyed far and wide from there. Several times he was captured by In-

dians. But he always managed to escape. He lived to be an old man.

Boone is buried in Frankfort, Ky. A monument to honor him stands at his grave. Some of the trails he blazed are monuments to him, too. They are marked so that they can be followed even today. (See PIONEER LIFE IN AMERICA.)

Daniel built a fort at Boonesborough.

BOSPORUS   A narrow strait called the Bosporus joins the Black Sea and the Sea of Marmara. Ships sailing between the Black Sea and the Mediterranean must go through the Bosporus.

This strait is about twenty miles long and from one-third of a mile to two miles wide. It is between Turkey in Europe and Turkey in Asia. The famous Turkish city of Istanbul lies on both sides of the southern end of the Bosporus. The modern part of Istanbul lies on the European shore. The older part of the city is on the Asian shore. The northern end of the strait has heavy fogs and dangerous currents. Because of them many lighthouses have been built there to aid the ships.

The name "Bosporus" comes from the Greek words meaning "ox" and "ford." Where the strait is narrowest, oxen could swim across. An old Greek myth tells that the beautiful maiden Io, after Zeus had changed her into a cow, swam the Bosporus to escape a gadfly.

At the opposite end of the Sea of Marmara is another strait—the Dardanelles. The Bosporus, the Sea of Marmara, and the Dardanelles together are sometimes called just "The Straits." (See BLACK SEA; DARDANELLES; ISTANBUL; STRAIT.)

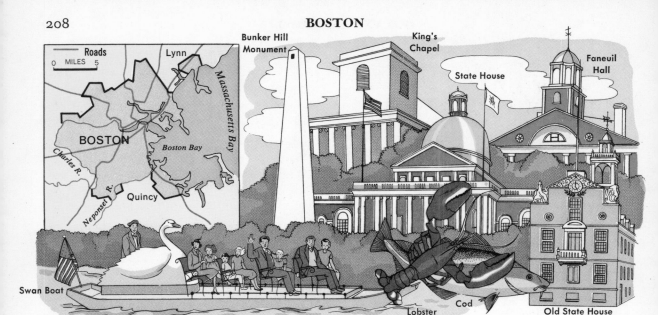

BOSTON The city of Boston is larger than any other city in New England. It is one of the 10 biggest cities in the whole United States. This big city is the capital of Massachusetts. The state house with its gold dome stands on Beacon Hill. It looks down over Boston Common, the oldest public park in the country.

Boston is a seaport with a good harbor. Ships come to it from ports all over the world. Hundreds of fishing boats go out from Boston and come back loaded with fish. One of the sights of the city is Fish Pier. There the fishermen unload their boats and sell the fish they have caught.

A jingle about Boston calls it "the home of the bean and the cod." Beans did not help to make Boston great, even though one way of baking beans is named for Boston. But cod did help the city grow. Since the early days, fishermen have gone out from Boston to fishing banks near Newfoundland and have brought back boatloads of cod.

Roads and railroads spread out from Boston to all other parts of New England. These roads and railroads helped Boston to grow, because they helped to make it a great market town. Wool, leather, textiles, and shoes are some of the things that are bought and sold there. Its many factories also helped to make Boston a big city.

Ever since its early days Boston has been famous for its schools. Many excellent colleges and universities are in or near it.

The city is not many miles from Plymouth Rock, where the Pilgrims landed. Boston began as a small town in 1630. The town was on a little peninsula joined to the mainland by only a narrow neck of land. The early settlers named their village Boston after a city in England. The streets in the old part of Boston are still narrow and crooked, just as they were in the early village. But Boston now has many wide and beautiful streets, too. The city has spread out far beyond the peninsula on which it started. Much of the land over which it has spread was made by filling in the sea.

Boston had an important part in the early history of the United States. The Boston Tea Party happened in Boston harbor. Paul Revere's famous ride to warn people that the British were coming started in Boston. The Battle of Bunker Hill was fought in what is now a part of Boston. And here much of the planning was done that led to the building of the new country.

There are many landmarks in Boston that tell of the part it has played in history. Thousands of people visit these landmarks every year. (See BUNKER HILL; MASSACHUSETTS; PILGRIMS; REVERE, PAUL.)

BOTANY The science of botany is the study of plants. Plants are very important. Without them people and other animals would have no food. Plants also furnish many things besides food.

Because plants are so important, we need to know a great many things about them. We need to know how they are built and how they carry on the work of living. We need to know how different plants manage to live in different soils and different climates and with different plant and animal neighbors. We need to know which plants are closely related. We need to know how to make plants grow well and how to get new and better kinds. We need to know, too, how to protect plants from disease and insect enemies. No wonder botany has been divided into many "smaller" sciences! (See PLANT BREEDING; PLANT KINGDOM.)

BOWLING The popular game of bowling is played with big pins and a big ball. Ten wooden pins weighing at least 3 1/2 pounds apiece are set up at one end of a smooth runway, or alley. The balls may weigh as much as 16 pounds and be 27 inches around. A player who finds a 16-pound ball too heavy may use a lighter one. But, of course, with a heavy ball a player has a better chance of knocking down the heavy pins.

There are ten rounds, or frames, in a game. In a frame each player is allowed to roll two balls. If he knocks all the pins down with the first ball, he has a "strike." If he knocks them all down with two balls, he has a "spare."

Scoring is rather complicated. The highest possible score in a game is 300. To get this the player must have a strike in every frame. Perfect games are not common, but neither are they rare.

Bowling was brought to the United States by early Dutch settlers. It was then called "skittles" and was played with nine pins instead of ten. The lawmakers thought that people were wasting too much time playing ninepins and passed a law against the game. But those who wanted to play soon found a way of getting around the law. They began using ten pins instead of nine.

This bowler has thrown a hook shot and made a perfect strike.

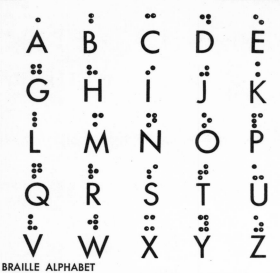

BRAILLE ALPHABET

Reading Braille

Cutting Braille Letters with Pointed Stylus

BRAILLE Blind people cannot read ordinary writing or printing because they cannot see. But a number of ways of writing for the blind have been worked out. The one most often used is Braille.

Braille is named for the Frenchman who invented it—Louis Braille. He himself was a blind man.

In Braille each letter is made of dots which are raised from the page. A blind person reads Braille by running his fingers over lines of dots. In reading, he must notice both the number of dots and how they are arranged. Several letters, for instance, are made of three dots, but the dots are not arranged the same way.

There are now books, newspapers, and magazines in Braille. Blind people no longer have to depend on other people to read to them what is going on in the world.

BRAIN A big airplane standing on a runway is a wonderful machine. But it cannot fly unless it has a pilot. Our bodies are wonderful machines, too. But they also have to have pilots to make them work. The pilots of our bodies are our brains.

Our brains are more than simple pilots. They do more than keep our body machines running and make them go where we want them to go. They also let us think and remember and build castles in the air.

A boy or girl who has been going to school for a few years knows the multiplication

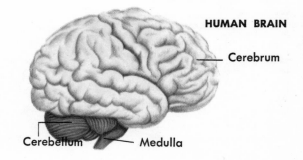

HUMAN BRAIN

— Cerebrum

Cerebellum   — Medulla

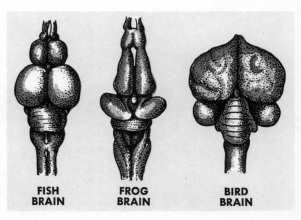

FISH BRAIN   FROG BRAIN   BIRD BRAIN

table and the alphabet. He knows a great many words. He has a great many ideas about a great many things. But his brain, if we could see it, would show no sign of what is stored in it. The brain is made up of cells just as every other part of the body is. The outer covering of much of it is gray. Saying that a person has a great deal of gray matter is another way of saying that he has a good brain.

The brain sends messages to the other parts of the body by way of the nerves. If a person wishes to stoop over to pick up a pin, the brain sends messages to muscles in the back. It also sends messages to muscles in the arms and fingers. It takes many messages for even so simple an action.

A person's brain has three main parts. The picture shows them.

The medulla (me DULL a) is connected with the big bundle of nerves we call the spinal cord. This part of the brain controls breathing and the beating of the heart.

The cerebellum (ser ee BELL um) helps make our muscles move smoothly. A person whose cerebellum has been injured moves in a jerky way.

The largest part of the brain is the cerebrum (SER ee brum). It is the part which

enables us to think and remember and imagine. It is the part that makes it possible for us to hear and talk. It makes it possible for us to see and smell and taste and feel what we touch. Even with excellent eyes and ears we could not see or hear if messages did not reach our cerebrums.

It is the cerebrum which is gray on the outside. The inside is white. There are many folds in the gray covering.

All mammals have brains somewhat like ours. The same parts are there. But we have especially big cerebrums. The gray covering, moreover, is much folded. In various ways we are far behind some of our mammal relatives. We are weaker than some and slower than others. But we are more intelligent than any other mammals because of our big cerebrums with their many folds.

We are even farther ahead of other animals with backbones. Birds have small cerebrums with no folds. Reptiles and amphibians have even smaller ones. In fishes the cerebrum is hardly noticeable.

Animals without backbones have no cerebrums. Some kinds of animals have no brains at all. (See BODY, HUMAN; INTELLIGENCE QUOTIENT.)

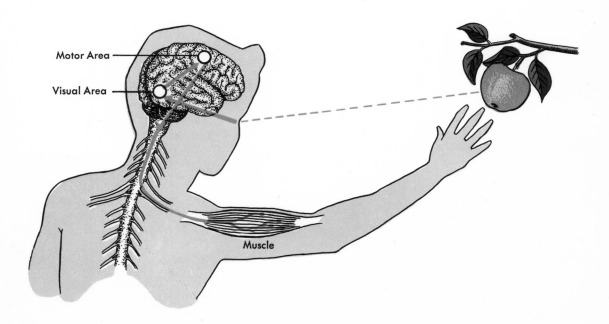

Motor Area

Visual Area

Muscle

BRAZIL

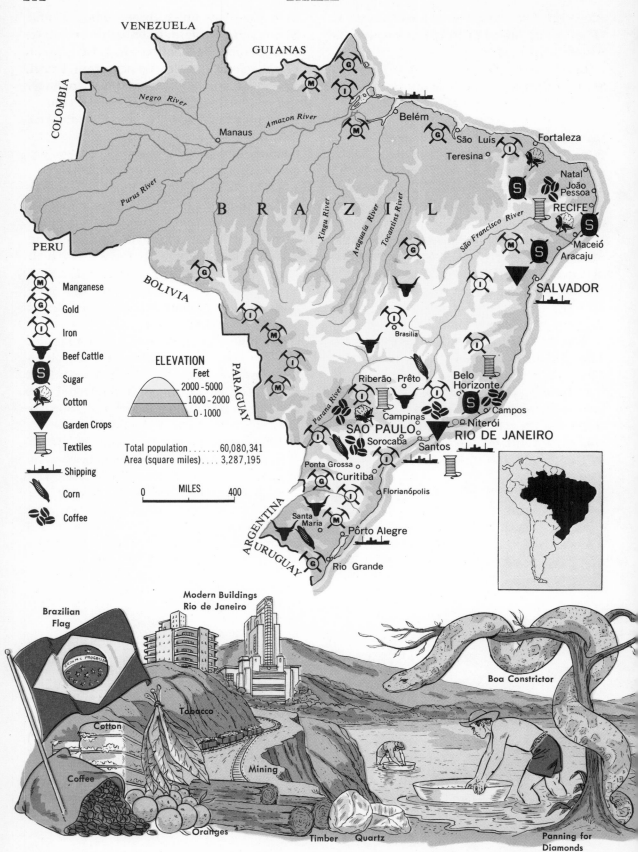

VENEZUELA

GUIANAS

COLOMBIA

Negro River

Manaus

Amazon River

Belém

São Luís

Fortaleza

Teresina

Natal

João Pessoa

RECIFE

Maceió

Aracaju

SALVADOR

PERU

Purus River

B R A Z I L

São Francisco River

BOLIVIA

Brasilia

Belo Horizonte

Campos

Riberão Prêto

Campinas

Niterói

SAO PAULO

RIO DE JANEIRO

Sorocaba

Santos

Ponta Grossa

Curitiba

Florianópolis

PARAGUAY

Parana River

Xingu River

Araguaia River

Tocantins River

ARGENTINA

URUGUAY

Santa Maria

Pôrto Alegre

Rio Grande

Legend

- M Manganese
- G Gold
- I Iron
- Beef Cattle
- S Sugar
- Cotton
- Garden Crops
- Textiles
- Shipping
- Corn
- Coffee

ELEVATION
Feet
2000 - 5000
1000 - 2000
0 - 1000

Total population 60,080,341
Area (square miles) 3,287,195

MILES
0   400

Illustrations

Brazilian Flag

Modern Buildings Rio de Janeiro

Boa Constrictor

Tobacco

Cotton

Coffee

Mining

Oranges

Timber

Quartz

Panning for Diamonds

BRAZIL The full name of this country is "The United States of Brazil." Usually it is just called Brazil.

Brazil is by far the largest country in South America. It is a little larger than the United States.

In 1500, just eight years after Columbus' first voyage to America, a Portuguese explorer landed at Brazil. Portuguese ships soon began trading with the Indians there. They got from the Indians a kind of red dyewood. The name Brazil came from the name of this wood.

Long before the Pilgrims landed at Plymouth there were Portuguese settlements in Brazil. The country now contains half the people of South America. Even so, Brazil has only one person for every three in the United States.

The equator crosses northern Brazil. This part of the country is hot and rainy. The Amazon flows across it just south of the equator. Heavy forests cover the region. Not many people live there. Most of those who do, make a living by gathering rubber and Brazil nuts from the forest.

The "bulge" of Brazil reaches far out into the Atlantic. In much of this land, hot-weather crops are raised. The chief ones are sugar cane, cacao, and cotton.

Farther south there is a region of cities and farms and mines. Rio de Janeiro and São Paulo, Brazil's two biggest cities, are here. Each has about three million people. The farms are plantations, or *fazendas,* on which coffee and cotton are raised. Much of the world's coffee comes from Brazil. The chief mines are iron and manganese mines. Brazil has "mountains" of iron.

Still farther south the climate is too cool for coffee and cotton. Corn, wheat, and potatoes are raised. There are ranches. Good lumber comes from the forests.

Deep inland and south of the Amazon valley, the land is high. Like the Amazon country, it is almost empty.

In 1958 the government completed the first buildings in Brasilia, a new city which many people believe will become the new capital of Brazil. Brasilia is on the great inland plateau about 600 miles northwest of Rio de Janeiro.

For more than 300 years Brazil was ruled by Portugal. But in 1822 the Brazilians won their independence and chose Dom Pedro as their emperor. His son, Dom Pedro II, followed him and ruled till 1889. In 1891 Brazil became a republic.

Portuguese is the language of Brazil. Many Brazilians are of Portuguese descent. There are some negroes whose ancestors were slaves. There are Indians whose ancestors were there when the white men came. And there are people from many lands. Brazil welcomes settlers. (See AMAZON RIVER; RIO DE JANEIRO.)

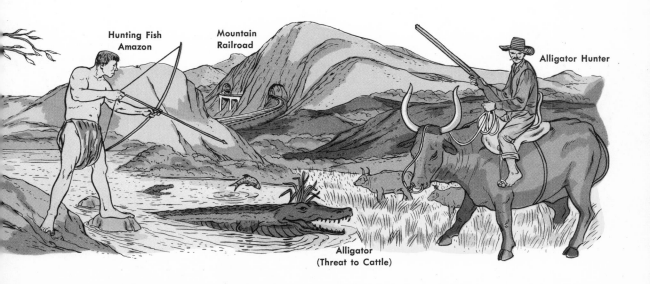

Hunting Fish
Amazon

Mountain
Railroad

Alligator Hunter

Alligator
(Threat to Cattle)

BREAD The people of every land have their own kinds of bread. But all bread is alike in one way. It is made of flour and a liquid. The flour, as a rule, comes from grain. But it can also be made from potatoes, soybeans, peas, breadfruit, bananas, or some kinds of roots.

Breads can be divided into two groups. Those in one group are light and more or less fluffy. They are raised, or leavened, breads. Others are thin and hard. They are unleavened breads.

One way of making bread light and fluffy is to put yeast in it. The yeast gives off little bubbles of carbon dioxide. These bubbles puff up the dough.

There are other ways of producing bubbles of carbon dioxide in bread dough. Baking powder can be used. So can sour milk and soda. Biscuits and other quick breads are made without yeast.

Matzoth is one kind of unleavened bread. Graham crackers are another.

Bread is a very important kind of food. It is sometimes called the "staff of life." Much of the bread we eat now is enriched. Vitamins and minerals have been added to it. Bread is so important that the word "bread" is sometimes used to stand for all our food. In the Lord's Prayer, when we say, "Give us this day our daily bread," we are really asking for all the food we need to keep us well and strong. (See CARBON DIOXIDE; FLOUR; YEASTS.)

Breadfruit is an important food in the tropics.

BREADFRUIT The Osage orange is a common tree in parts of the United States. Farmers used to plant hedges of it on their farms. This tree bears fruits that look like green oranges. People often call them hedge apples. Hedge apples are pretty, but they are not good to eat. The Osage orange, however, has a cousin that bears big orange-shaped fruits that *are* good to eat. This cousin is the breadfruit tree.

From its name it is easy to guess that bread can be made from its fruits. The fruits are not sweet like oranges and apples. Instead, they are starchy, like potatoes. If bread is to be made from it, a breadfruit is first sliced and dried. Then it is pounded up into flour. A breadfruit may also be roasted whole.

The breadfruit tree grows only in very warm, wet lands. It is found chiefly on islands in the South Pacific. If a native of one of these islands is sitting under a breadfruit tree, his dinner may drop into his lap.

There are different kinds of breadfruit. Some kinds ripen at one time of year, some at another. In places where the trees grow, there is usually breadfruit to eat all the year around.

BREADS OF THE WORLD

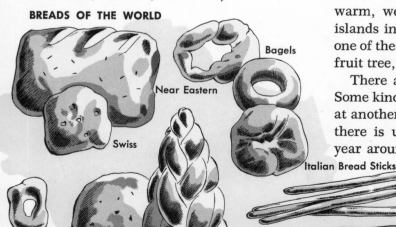

Bagels

Near Eastern

Swiss

Italian Bread Sticks

American Breads

French

Russian Kringel-Baranki

European Rye

Slovakian Plaited

BREATHING All animals breathe. They breathe in oxygen, one of the gases the air is made of. Some animals get oxygen directly from the air itself. Some get it from air that is dissolved in water. All animals, as they breathe out, throw carbon dioxide away.

Different animals breathe in different ways. People and all other mammals breathe with lungs. So do all birds and reptiles and most grown-up amphibians. Lungs are made of tiny air sacs joined by little tubes.

All fishes have gills for breathing. Gills are small fringes or sheets of thin "skin." As water flows past them, the gills take in oxygen from the air dissolved in the water. Lungfishes have both gills and lungs. They can breathe either in or out of water.

Some baby insects that live in water have gills just as fishes do. Grown-up in-

Every type of animal must breathe.

sects have air tubes. Air travels through the tubes all over the insects' bodies.

Some spiders have air tubes. Others have book lungs. Book lungs are sacs filled with flaps of thin skin like the pages of a book.

Many animals have no special kind of breathing system. The earthworm is one of them. To breathe, it must be in moist soil. Oxygen from the air can then pass into the earthworm's body through its moist skin.

Some animals breathe much faster than others. A tiny pygmy shrew breathes ten times as fast as a person. But breathing, whether it is fast or slow, must not stop. Animals must have oxygen to stay alive. (See AIR; BLOOD; BODY, HUMAN; CARBON DIOXIDE; IRON LUNG; OXYGEN.)

BRICK For thousands of years people have made brick for building. Most of the bricks of long ago were sun-dried. They were made of mud, usually with straw mixed in to help hold the mud together. But by 5,000 years ago brickmakers also knew how to make much harder bricks by baking them in an oven instead of drying them in the sun.

Today sun-dried brick is still used in many parts of the world. But what most people mean by brick now is brick that has been made in an oven. An oven for making bricks is called a "kiln" (KILL).

The mud for brick is clay mixed with water. Some sand is added, too. The mud may be pressed into separate brick molds or made into long strips and then cut into bricks. The bricks are first dried. Then they are "fired." The temperature in a brick kiln may be over 2,000° F. The bricks are very hard when they leave the kiln. "As hard as a brick" is a common saying.

There are different kinds of "fired" brick. Glazed brick and firebrick are two of them. Glazed brick has a coating that makes it as smooth as glass. Firebrick contains much silica, which makes it stand fire well.

Termites do not eat brick. Fire cannot destroy it. Wind and weather do not make it rot. Buildings made of brick last a long time. (See BUILDING MATERIALS.)

Brickmaking is a very ancient craft.

Golden Gate Bridge

BRIDGES One day, thousands of years ago, one of our early ancestors wanted to cross a stream. He did not want to climb down the steep bank and wade through the cold water. On the bank he saw a dead tree that was leaning over. With his stone ax the man chopped at its base until it toppled across the stream. For the first time a man had made a bridge.

This story is made up. But it is a safe guess that the first man-made bridge was a log. No one can tell the true story of the first bridge because people learned how to make bridges long before they learned how to write about what they had done.

Now men know how to make many kinds of bridges. Some of them are among the wonders of today.

The pictures show several different kinds of bridges. Some bridges stay in place all the time. Some can be moved so that boats can pass. Some are meant to last for only a little while.

One bridge may be a combination of different kinds. One of the longest bridges in the world is the bridge that joins San Francisco and Oakland. For part of the way it is a suspension bridge. Then there is a cantilever (KAN ti lee ver) span. Next come several truss spans. The rest of the bridge is a continuous span.

Only small bridges are made of wood. Covered wooden bridges were once common in the United States. Now they are rare. All big bridges and most small ones built now are made of stone, concrete, or steel. The biggest bridges of today could not have been built without steel.

A big bridge has to be planned very carefully. It must have very solid foundations. It must be strong enough to stand the weight of the loads that will go across it. It must also be able to stand the swaying caused by the wind. The builder has to understand, too, that steel and the other materials big bridges are made of expand, or get bigger, when they are heated.

Most of the world's longest bridges are suspension bridges. The first really big

Some bridges have to be able to move so that they will not block traffic on the river.

Rope Bridge
Viaduct
Arcade Bridge
Wooden Covered Bridge
Cantilever Bridge
Arch Bridge
Continuous Span Bridge
Suspension Bridge
Vertical Lift
Drawbridge

suspension bridge ever built was New York's Brooklyn Bridge. It reaches across the East River. This bridge was finished in 1883.

Now the greatest of the suspension bridges is the Golden Gate Bridge. It reaches from San Francisco across the Golden Gate. From supporting tower to supporting tower this bridge is 4,200 feet long. The towers that hold it up are fixed on bedrock. They reach up 746 feet above the water. The main cables are a little more than a yard across. Each one is made of 27,572 separate wires about as big around as a lead pencil. There are 80,000 miles of wire in the two cables. On a hot day the cables expand and get longer. On a cold day

they contract and shorten. The floor of this great bridge is 20 feet higher at some times than at other times.

One of the world's two longest cantilever bridges is near Quebec, Canada. The other is over the Firth of Forth in Scotland. The two longest steel arch bridges are those at Bayonne, N. J., and Sydney, Australia.

Some bridges are famous for other things besides their length. The Bridge of Sighs in Venice is one. London Bridge is another. There are many more. Telling the whole story of bridges and their part in the history of the world would take many more pages than there are in this book. (See AQUEDUCT; BUILDING MATERIALS; CONCRETE; IRON AND STEEL.)

BRITISH EMPIRE Four hundred years ago Elizabeth I was the queen of England. In those days all Europe, it seemed, was going exploring. The great New World had been discovered. Elizabeth sent her sailors exploring, too. They carried the flag of England far and wide. Their work was the beginning of the British Empire, the biggest empire the world has ever seen.

"The sun never sets on the British Empire" is an old saying. British lands still stretch around the world. There are British lands on every continent. In size these lands vary greatly. Gibraltar is only a rocky point of land at the southern tip of Spain. Australia is a whole continent.

Britain built up her great empire partly by sending out settlers to form colonies in new lands. She fought wars for some of it. She bought small areas of her empire from other countries.

The colonies which became the United States were once a part of the British Empire. Britain lost them in the American Revolution. There have been many later changes in the Empire, too. In recent times some parts of it have broken away completely. Burma and the Republic of Ireland are among them. Other parts have won their independence but are members of the British Commonwealth of Nations, the name now given to all British lands.

The Commonwealth includes, besides Britain itself, these independent countries: Australia, Canada, Ceylon, the Federation of Malaya, Ghana, New Zealand, Pakistan, the Republic of India, and the Union of South Africa. In the Commonwealth there are also many colonies and other areas which are ruled at least in part by Britain.

Just the names of all the British lands would take a whole page the size of this one. Among the small but mighty places in this big empire are Malta, Hong Kong, Aden, and Singapore. (See ENGLAND; ENGLAND'S HISTORY; ENGLISH LANGUAGE; UNITED KINGDOM.)

BRITISH ISLES More than 5,500 islands make up the British Isles. There are two large islands, Great Britain and Ireland. The other islands are all small.

One group of the small islands is called the Shetland Islands. Shetland ponies came from there. The Channel Islands form another group. They are in the English Channel, between England and France. These islands are famous for their dairy cattle.

Phoenician and Greek ships reached the British Isles before the time of Christ. So did Roman armies. But not till less than a thousand years ago did the islands begin to play a really important part in the affairs of the world.

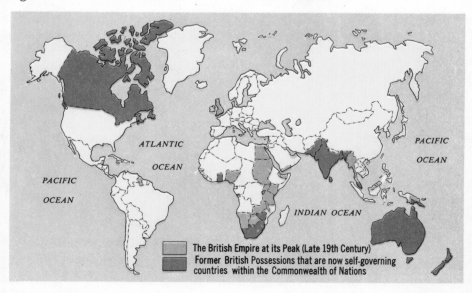

The British Empire at its Peak (Late 19th Century)
Former British Possessions that are now self-governing countries within the Commonwealth of Nations

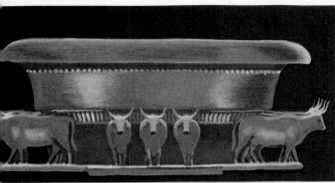

Side View

A huge bronze basin, called the "Sea of Bronze," stood in Solomon's temple. It held 10,000 gallons of water. Giant bronze bulls faced the four points of the compass.

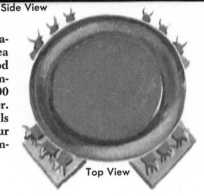

Top View

BRONZE The alloy called bronze is a mixture of copper and tin. Bronze has been used for at least 5,000 years—much longer than iron.

People of the Old Stone Age used tools and weapons made of stone. In the New Stone Age they had much better stone weapons. When copper was discovered, our early ancestors began making tools of copper. But copper was not hard enough to take the place of stone entirely.

Probably bronze was first made by accident. Some rocks have in them both copper ore and tin ore. When early man discovered bronze, he found it was much harder than copper. Early man learned to use bronze for tools and weapons. Later it was found that iron made even better tools and weapons. Iron gradually took the place of bronze.

The time when people used bronze for tools and weapons is called the Bronze Age. The Bronze Age came at different times in different parts of the world. The early civilizations of the Near East were in their Bronze Age more than 4,000 years ago. The Indians of South America were still in their Bronze Age when Columbus reached the New World less than 500 years ago.

Today many beautiful bowls and statues and doors are made of bronze. Much hardware is made of it. Bronze is used in bells, too. One big use of bronze in the United States is for pennies.

Things made of bronze last for a very long time. Bronze can stand heat and cold, wind and rain, and much handling. It lasts so well that it is sometimes called the "eternal metal." (See ALLOYS.)

BRUCE, ROBERT (1274-1329). A king of Scotland, Robert I, is a great Scottish hero. He is better known as Robert Bruce. Bruce led his people in a war that won for them freedom from England.

Bruce was crowned king in 1306. The English king did not want Scotland to have a king of its own. He went to war against Bruce and defeated him. But a few months later Bruce took the English by surprise and won a victory. Still the English king would not say that Bruce had a right to the throne. Battle after battle was fought. The most famous was the Battle of Bannockburn, which Bruce fought and won in 1314. His comrade-in-arms, another Scottish hero, was Lord James Douglas, nicknamed the Black Douglas. After Bannockburn the English king gave up his claim to Scotland. (See SCOTLAND.)

Robert Bruce was a daring warrior.

BUDDHA One of the world's great religions is Buddhism. Many millions of the people of Asia are Buddhists. They follow the teachings of Buddha.

Buddha lived about 2,500 years ago, five centuries before Christ. This great leader was born in India. His father was a king. His mother was the daughter of a king. The boy was named Siddhartha Gautama. Later he was called Buddha. "Buddha" means "Enlightened One."

Buddha had a happy boyhood. He lived in a palace and was not allowed to see how sad the lives of the poor people round about were. He married when he was 19, but he and his young wife went on living in the palace, shut off from the rest of the world.

It was not until Buddha was 29 that he found out that there was a great deal of suffering in the world. He decided then to give up his life of ease. He would try to help people bear their sorrows.

Buddha went into the mountains. Little by little he worked out his ideas of what people should believe and how they should live. After several years in the mountains Buddha came down to the crowded plains. For 45 years he went among the people teaching them to be kind and to bear their sorrows meekly. He was greatly loved.

In the cities of Asia today there are thousands of Buddhist temples. There are statues of Buddha in every one. (See RELIGIONS OF THE WORLD.)

BUENOS AIRES In August of 1534 a large band of Spaniards set sail for the New World. The king of Spain was sending them to found a settlement in the part of South America which is now Argentina. With them they had horses, cattle, plows, seeds, and household goods.

The ships sailed from Spain late in the summer. They sailed for five months. But it was still late summer when they ended their journey. For summer comes in Argentina when it is winter north of the equator.

The colonists reached the broad river called the Rio de la Plata. Flat grassland with grass as high as their heads stretched away from the river as far as they could see. The land along the river was swampy. But soon they came to a place that was higher. They landed there.

One of the settlers, as he stepped from his small, crowded boat, cried, "Santa Maria, what good air this is!" In this way the new settlement got its name, Buenos Aires. Buenos Aires means "good air."

The settlers had many troubles. Some died of disease. Some starved. Many were

Buenos Aires has more than 3,000,000 people.

killed by Indians. At last the settlement was moved far up the river where the Indians were friendly.

Forty years later some of the settlers came back down the river. They realized that this new country could not grow without a port city. And so Buenos Aires was born again. It became the largest city south of the equator, and the capital of Argentina.

It is no wonder that Buenos Aires grew large. It is a hundred miles from the ocean itself, but the Rio de la Plata is so wide and deep that ocean vessels can reach the city easily. Stretching away from it are thousands of square miles of some of the best farming land in the world. From it railroads fan out over the whole country. Many boats come down to it by way of the Paraná and Uruguay rivers. The trains and boats bring cattle and wheat and corn, cotton and sugar and wine. They carry back goods brought from all over the world.

Buenos Aires does not have the beautiful setting that Rio de Janeiro, the big city of Brazil, has. All the land in the city is level. Some of the older streets are narrow. The Spaniards made them narrow so that they would be shady. But many of the newer streets are broad and handsome. The city is especially proud of one very wide avenue, the wonderful Avenida Nueve de Julio.

Along the newer streets there are many beautiful buildings. Some of the fine homes look like homes in Spain. Some look like homes in Italy, for many thousands of Italians have come to this big city.

The city has plazas, as many cities of southern Europe do. It has five subways, the only ones in South America. On the outskirts there are factories. Most of them are meat-packing plants.

Some of the people of Buenos Aires work in the factories. But most of the work done in the city has to do with trade. So long as Argentina sells great amounts of goods to other lands and buys much goods from abroad, Buenos Aires will be one of the world's great cities. (See ARGENTINA.)

BUFFALO BILL (William F. Cody, 1846-1917) Half a century ago there were no western movies and television shows to watch. But when Buffalo Bill's famous Wild West show came to town, the people could crowd into a big circus tent and see real Indians and cowboys of the old West. Indians in war paint riding bareback on their western ponies and shouting war whoops thundered into the ring. Behind them came buckskinned cowboys shooting as they rode. Buffalo Bill himself was the star of the show. He performed amazing tricks with his guns.

William Cody was born in Iowa, but his family soon moved to Kansas. When he was only 14 he was hired as a rider for the Pony Express. He learned to know the Great Plains well. He knew both the land and the Indians who lived on it. Before long he became a scout for the army and helped fight the Indians.

Buffalo Bill got his nickname because he killed so many "buffaloes," or bison. When the Kansas Pacific Railroad was being built across the plains, young Cody agreed to furnish the workmen with meat. In one year he killed nearly 5,000 bison.

In 1883 he gathered many Indians and cowboys together and started his Wild West show. People liked it so much that he traveled about with it for many years.

The town of Cody, Wyo., was named for Buffalo Bill. (See BISON, AMERICAN.)

AMBUSH BUG

BUGS Many people call all insects bugs. All bugs are insects, but not all insects are bugs. Even some of the insects that have "bug" in their names are not true bugs. The lightning bug, the ladybug, the June bug, and the potato bug are not bugs. They are beetles. The true bugs make up only one of the many groups, or orders, of insects.

True bugs have transparent outer wings that overlap a little at the tip. Their legs are long and slim. They have mouth parts with which they can pierce a plant or an animal and suck out the juices.

Some bugs have names that fit them very well. The squash bug sucks the juice from squash plants. The assassin bug kills many other insects. The ambush bug lies in am-

bush among leaves and flowers and watches for insects it can catch. The toad bug looks as warty as a toad and goes hopping about in search of food.

Not all bugs live on land. Water boatmen look like tiny boats as they swim about on the surface of the water. Back swimmers swim on their backs. Water striders slide over the surface of water on their slender legs. Giant water bugs are true giants as compared with other bugs.

Most bugs do little or no harm. A few do some good. The assassin bug, for example, eats many grasshoppers and potato beetles. But some are our enemies. The chinch bug, for instance, does a great deal of damage to our crops. (See INSECT PESTS; INSECTS.)

BUILDING MATERIALS The buildings in the picture are made of many different materials. The house being built is a frame house. It is made of wood, as all frame houses are. The Indian house is made of adobe (a DOE bee), or sun-dried brick. The outside walls of the hotel are fired brick. The walls of the Capitol Building are stone. So are the walls of the small cottage. The cottage roof is thatched—made of grass.

BACKSWIMMER
0.5"

WATER-
BOATMAN
0.4"

WATER STRIDERS   0.4"

GIANT WATER
BUG 2.2"

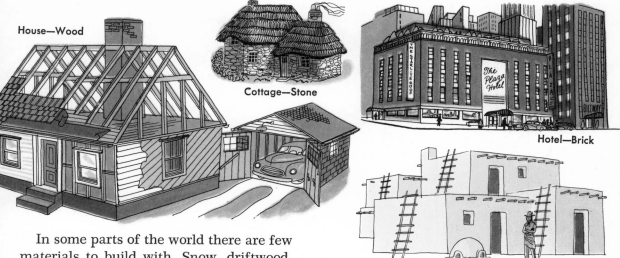

House—Wood

Cottage—Stone

Hotel—Brick

Lodge—Adobe

Capitol—Stone

In some parts of the world there are few materials to build with. Snow, driftwood, walrus skin, and sod, for instance, are about all an Eskimo can find for building. But in the United States and many other countries, too, there are numerous materials to choose from. We can choose from more than a dozen materials for the outside walls. Many other materials can be used for roofs and floors and inside walls, for pipes and gutters and built-in furniture.

Stone is a natural building material. It has only to be cut into the shape wanted. There are dozens of kinds of stone. Those used most in building are limestone, marble, granite, sandstone, and slate. Sometimes the stone is not even cut into shape. Rounded stones called field stones make attractive walls.

Wood is another natural building material. There are many kinds of wood to choose from. Pine and oak are common.

Snow, grass, palm leaves, and mud are natural building materials, too. No one had to invent them.

But many of our building materials are man-made. They had to be invented. Brick, steel, glass, concrete, plywood, fiber board, and plaster are a few of them.

Some of the materials used in our buildings do not show after the buildings are finished. In many walls, for instance, rock wool is used to shut heat in during the winter and keep heat out during the sum-

mer. It does not show. In the same way, no one would guess to look at the great Empire State Building in New York City that a framework made of 57,000 tons of steel is hidden in its walls.

There are many things to think about in choosing the materials for a building. Here are five: How will they look? How long will they last? How much will they cost? How easy are they to keep in repair? Are they fireproof?

Buildings, of course, are not the only things we build. We also build bridges and tunnels and dams. We build roadways and canal locks and piers. Here again there are many materials to choose from. Here again there are many questions to answer in deciding which ones to use. (See ARCHITECTURE; BRICK; BRIDGES; CONCRETE; DAMS; HOMES; ROCKS; SKYSCRAPERS; WOOD.)

Paper-white
Narcissus
Bulb

Dried Bulb

Cutaway View

Bulb Sprouting

BULBS Many plants are raised from bulbs. In the center of a bulb there is a baby plant. Most of the bulb is made up of thick leaves in which food for the baby plant is stored. It is easy to pull away the leaves and find the little plant inside.

Tulips and daffodils are usually raised from bulbs. So are many other spring flowers. Some bulbs will grow indoors in winter even if they are planted in nothing but water and pebbles. The paper-white narcissus is probably the easiest plant to raise in this way. One of our common vegetables is a bulb. It is the onion.

BULGARIA The country of Bulgaria is in the Balkan Peninsula in southeastern Europe. The famous Danube River flows along its northern border. Much of the country is mountainous. But there are low-lands where the soil is excellent and big crops can be raised.

Most of the people of Bulgaria are farmers. They raise chiefly livestock, grain, cotton, sugar, and tobacco. Bulgaria is famous for its roses. These roses are raised for their perfume. Most of the world's attar, or oil, of roses comes from Bulgaria.

There are stores of minerals in the country. But there is not much mining. And there are not many factories.

Bulgaria has a seacoast on the Black Sea but no very large seaports. Its only really big city is the capital, Sofia. On the whole Bulgaria is backward, but Sofia has many fine streets and modern buildings.

Bulgaria is a crossroads country. Its low-lands make easy routes between central Europe and Asia. As one would expect, one finds there a mixture of East and West.

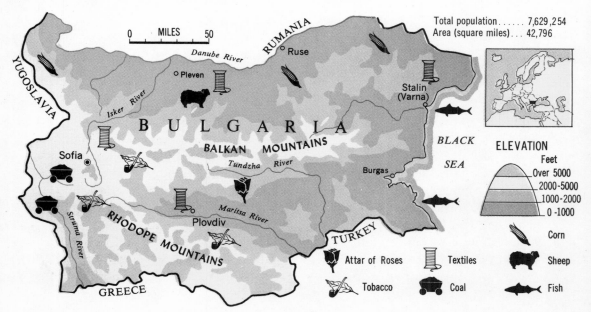

Total population......7,629,254
Area (square miles)...42,796

ELEVATION
Feet
Over 5000
2000-5000
1000-2000
0 -1000

Corn
Sheep
Fish

Attar of Roses   Textiles
Tobacco   Coal

Bulgarian Flag
Sheepherding
Gathering Roses For Rose Oil
Ancient Turkish Minaret
Tobacco
Oxen Plowing

Bulgaria has been a battlefield many times. For almost five centuries Bulgaria was under the domination of the Turks. Now it is independent and has a government much like that of the Soviet Union. Bulgaria's trade is mostly with its next-door neighbors and the Soviet Union.

BUNKER HILL The Battle of Bunker Hill was the first big battle of the Revolutionary War. It was fought on June 17, 1775. Actually, the battle was fought not on Bunker Hill, but on nearby Breed's Hill. The Bunker Hill monument that marks the place of the battle is on Breed's Hill.

Both Bunker Hill and Breed's Hill are in Charlestown, which is now a part of Boston. In the days of the Revolution, Charlestown was a separate city. On June 16, 1775, the British were holding Boston. That night American soldiers were sent up Breed's Hill to dig trenches. The trenches would be a protection from cannon fire from British ships in the harbor. The Americans could then use their own guns to fire down on the British in Boston.

The next morning the British saw what had been done. At once British troops stormed the hill. The American colonel, William Prescott, gave his famous command, "Don't fire until you can see the whites of their eyes." Many of the British soldiers were killed. The British attacked again. Again many were killed. Then the Americans ran out of gunpowder. At their third try the British captured the hill. Even though they lost the battle, the Americans were given courage. They had made the British lose more than one-third of their 2,400 men to win the victory.

Burbank developed a spineless cactus.

BURBANK, LUTHER (1849-1926) Because of the many new kinds of plants he produced, Luther Burbank is often called a "plant wizard." He carried on thousands of experiments with plants. In his very first one he produced the Burbank potato, an especially large and firm potato. From this new kind of potato Burbank made enough money to let him move from New England to California, where the climate was better for his experiments.

The plumcot, the Shasta daisy, and the spineless cactus are three of Burbank's plant inventions. He spent 16 years getting the spineless cactus—a cactus plant that could be used as cattle food. He called this new plant his greatest work.

Of course, not all Burbank's experiments turned out well. He often had big bonfires to burn up plants that were not worth saving. His neighbors called them "ten-thousand-dollar bonfires" because in them the work of months or even years was being burned up. But so many of his experiments were a success that visitors came from all over the world to see and talk with him. (See HYBRIDS; PLANT BREEDING.)

BURMA Across the big Bay of Bengal from India is the country of Burma. Burma once was a part of the British Empire, but in 1948 it became independent. It is a land of heat and heavy rains, of elephants and water buffaloes, of rice fields and dense forests.

The biggest city of Burma is Rangoon. Rangoon is on the great delta of the Irrawaddy River. Part of this delta is good farmland. Part of it is covered with mangrove swamps. Rangoon is about 20 miles from the coast. Big ocean boats can reach it by way of the Irrawaddy.

About 400 miles farther up the river from Rangoon is Mandalay, Burma's next-largest city. Kipling made this city famous by his poem "On the Road to Mandalay."

Burma is about the size of Texas but has more than twice as many people. Most of the people live near the rivers or the coasts. They are chiefly farmers and fishermen. The farmers use water buffaloes to help in the rice fields. Some of Burma's people

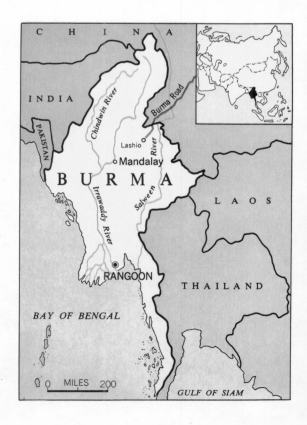

work in her oil fields. Others work in her forests. Burma exports rice, oil, and teak. Teak is a hard yellowish-brown wood that does not rot easily. Elephants push the heavy teak logs to the rivers. Then the logs are floated to the sawmills.

Burma was in the news often during World War II. For a while, the only way the Allies had of getting supplies into China was by the famous 800-mile-long Burma Road. (See KIPLING, RUDYARD.)

Churning Butter By Hand

Modern Packaged Butter

BUTTER All milk has some fat in it. Butter is made from this fat. Butter as we buy it is mostly fat. But some water from the milk is still left in it, and usually a little salt has been added as seasoning. More important, butter has in it some of the vitamins we need to keep us well.

Butter is made by churning milk or cream. Cream is the part of the milk that is richest in butterfat. In a churn the milk or cream is shaken about. During the shaking the tiny particles of fat in the milk come together and form lumps. These lumps are then worked into butter.

The butter used in the United States is made from cow's milk. But butter can be made from the milk of other animals. In Tibet, for example, it is made from the milk of the yak. In many countries it comes from the milk of goats or sheep.

People have known how to make butter for thousands of years. They may have found out how by accident. The first churning was probably done by shaking milk in a bag of skin. (See FOODS; MILK.)

BUTTERFLIES AND MOTHS There are more than half a million kinds of insects. Thousands of these kinds of insects are moths or butterflies.

Moths and butterflies have six legs. They would not be insects if they did not. Their bodies are divided into three regions, as the bodies of all insects are. They have feelers, as all insects do. But in one way moths and butterflies are different from all other insects. They have scales on their wings. These scales lap over one another like the shingles on a roof. It is not always easy to tell whether a "scale-wing" is a moth or a butterfly. Here are a few helps:

Butterflies usually fly in the daytime. They flit about in our gardens on sunny summer days. Moths as a rule fly at night.

Butterflies usually hold their wings up when they are resting. Moths usually hold theirs flat or in a rooflike position.

The body of a butterfly is slender. As a rule the body of a moth is plump. It often looks furry.

The feelers are the best help of all. A butterfly has slender feelers with a thicker part, or club, at the end. A moth's feelers

ANTENNAS

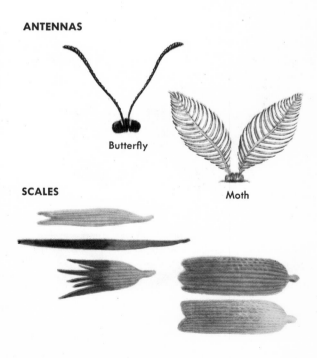

Butterfly

Moth

SCALES

may be like threads, or they may be like tiny feathers.

All the insects in the pictures on this page are butterflies. All those on the next page are moths.

There are four stages in the life of every moth and butterfly. These four stages are egg, larva, pupa, and adult.

The larva of a moth or butterfly is often called a caterpillar. Caterpillars eat a great deal and grow fast. They grow so fast that they actually grow out of their skins. They may shed their skins several times. A caterpillar's new skin may be quite different in color from the old skin it just crawled out of.

The pupa stage is the sleepy stage. The insect does not move about or eat. Many moths spend this stage in a cocoon. The cocoon is made of silken threads which the caterpillar spins when it is ready to become a pupa. Butterflies do not spin cocoons. A butterfly pupa is often called a chrysalis. While the moth or butterfly is a pupa, great changes take place. It is hard to believe that the four-winged insect that finally flies away was once a crawling caterpillar.

Some "scale-wings" eat nothing at all after they are grown up. Of course, they

BUTTERFLIES

Bronze Copper

Gulf Fritillary

Spring Azure

Mourning Cloak

Monarch

Chrysalis

Larva

Elm Leaf

Eggs

Monarch Larva on Milkweed

Chrysalis

Tiger Swallowtail

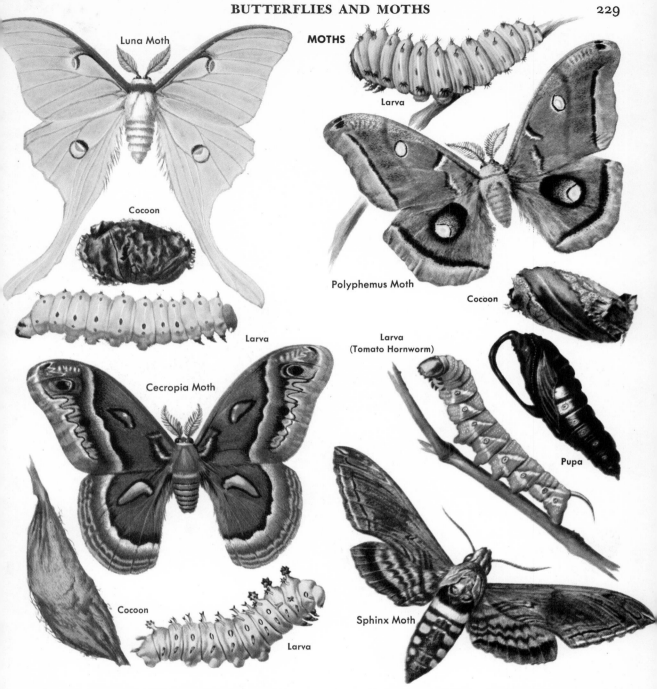

MOTHS

Luna Moth

Larva

Cocoon

Larva

Polyphemus Moth

Cocoon

Larva
(Tomato Hornworm)

Cecropia Moth

Pupa

Cocoon

Larva

Sphinx Moth

do not live long. Others drink nectar from flowers. These help us by carrying pollen from flower to flower as they are getting the nectar.

Caterpillars, on the other hand, often do a great deal of harm. They are very big eaters, and many of them eat things that we are not willing to let them have. Some eat the leaves of trees. Some eat fruits and vegetables. Some eat holes in our rugs or clothes. Most of the caterpillars that do great harm are the caterpillars of moths. The cabbage worm is an exception. It is the caterpillar of the pretty cabbage butterfly. There is one good thing to be said for caterpillars. Silk comes from the cocoons spun by the caterpillars of the silkworm moth. (See INSECT PESTS; INSECTS.)

BUTTONS Today buttons are so common that it is hard to think of not having them. But people had beautiful clothes of silks and satins and velvets long before buttons were used as fasteners. To fasten their clothes, the people of early times used strings, sashes, and pins. There were buttons even in very ancient times, but they were used only as decoration. The first buttons known to have been used as fasteners were made in the days of the famous Queen Elizabeth I of England.

All early buttons, whether they were used as fasteners or as decoration, were expensive. They had to be made by hand. Many of them were of gold or silver. Some had jewels set in them. Some were even carved out of jewels.

Many buttons are still used just for decoration. And some are still expensive. In fact, the buttons on a dress may cost more than the cloth the dress is made of. But there are now cheap buttons, too. Buttons can be made cheaply today because they can be manufactured by machine.

Today's buttons are made of many different materials. Shell, wood, leather, cloth, and glass are a few of them. Bone, horses' hoof, vegetable ivory, brass, silver, and steel are others. The newest materials for buttons are plastics. Buttons are made in a great many colors and sizes and shapes, too.

Now other kinds of fasteners, such as zippers, hooks-and-eyes, and snaps, have partly taken the place of buttons. Buttons, however, are sure to be used for many years to come.

Buttons come in many shapes, sizes, and materials.

Byrd's plane flew over the rocks and ice of Antarctica.

BYRD, RICHARD EVELYN (1888-1957) The most famous American explorer of modern times, Richard E. Byrd, gave signs at an early age of what he would be when he grew up. At the age of 12 he took a trip by himself around the world.

In 1925 Byrd went on a polar expedition to Greenland. What he learned there made him sure that an airplane would be able to fly over the North Pole. The following year he, with Floyd Bennett as the pilot, set out from Spitsbergen to fly to the Pole 680 miles away. Airplanes in 1926 were not nearly as reliable as they are today. But the two explorers made the trip safely. They were the first men ever to make a flight over the North Pole.

Three years later Byrd set out from a base on the Ross Ice Shelf in Antarctica and became the first man ever to fly over the South Pole. He claimed a great amount of Antarctica for the United States.

On several expeditions to Antarctica, the last in 1956, Byrd mapped 450,000 square miles of this icy continent. He spent many months alone studying its harsh climate.

Twice Byrd almost lost his life on adventures. A plane in which he was flying across the Atlantic was forced down at sea in 1927. In 1934 gas fumes from a stove almost killed him in a hut in Antarctica. Many movies and books tell of Byrd's experiences. (See ANTARCTICA.)

The letter C looks much like G. There is a good reason why. Once C and G were simply two ways of writing the same letter.

This letter probably began as the picture of a camel. When the Greeks took it into their alphabet, they wrote it in first one way and then another (⌐ ┌). The Romans, when it came to them, also wrote it in two ways (C G). In time the two ways of writing it became two different letters.

C has different sounds. Its sound in *cat* is not like its sound in *ceiling* or *ocean*. Two c's together, as in *success*, may not sound alike. In some words like *scene*, c is silent.

CABLES, SUBMARINE The first telegraph line was opened in 1844. Soon there were thousands of miles of telegraph lines on land. And before long people could send telegraph messages across oceans. Sending these messages was made possible by the laying of heavy wires, or cables, across the seas from continent to continent. Cables laid under the sea are called submarine cables. The telegraph messages sent over them are called cablegrams.

The Atlantic was the first ocean to be crossed by cable. After several failures, Cyrus W. Field, an American, succeeded in 1866 in laying a cable from Newfoundland to Ireland. The Pacific Ocean was spanned with a cable 36 years later.

In 1955 a telephone cable was laid across the Atlantic. Since then other telephone cables have been laid. Such cables make it possible to hear someone across the sea as clearly as if he were just across town.

The wire through which the electricity flows is only a small part of a submarine cable. The wire must have waterproof covering, because salt water is a fairly good conductor of electricity. The wire must be protected against sharp rocks, dragging anchors, and swordfish. The cable must be so strong that it will not break of its own weight as it is being lowered to its place at the bottom of the sea. The cable also must have an outside layer that shipworms cannot bore through.

All of the world's undersea cables together now measure more than 400 thousand miles. They really girdle the globe. (See TELEGRAPH; TELEPHONE.)

PARTS OF A SUBMARINE CABLE

Electric Wire
Copper Tape
Rubber
Alloy Tape
Soft Rubber
Cushion
Steel Armor Wires
Tarred Jute

CACTI The cacti make up a rather big family of flowering plants. There are about 1,000 kinds. They vary greatly in size and shape. Some are as tall as a house; others are no bigger than a thimble. Some are as round and squatty as a tub while others twine their way through trees like very long, thorny snakes.

The cactus family is one of the truly American plant families. There are now cactus plants in other parts of the world, but they all came in the beginning from the Americas.

Many people think of deserts when they hear the word "cactus." Not all cacti live in deserts, but most of them do. Desert cacti are sometimes called the heroes of the plant world because they can stand heat and dryness that would kill most plants. The cacti pictured live in the deserts of southwestern United States. All these cacti have good roots for taking in water after a rain. They also have several ways of keeping the water they take in from evaporating. Their green stems must do the work that leaves do for most green plants. Having no leaves cuts down the chance for the water taken in to evaporate. A coating of wax on the stems helps hold in water, too. Their stems are big enough to be good storage tanks. And they are fluted so they can expand and contract easily.

Raising cacti is a popular hobby. People like them for their strange shapes. Besides, cactus flowers are beautiful. They come in many colors—yellow, orange, scarlet, pink, and purple. No cactus has flowers more beautiful or fragrant than the night-blooming cereus. Its flowers are pure white. A flower is open for only one night. When this cactus is in bloom people gather from miles around to see it. (See ADAPTATION TO ENVIRONMENT; BURBANK, LUTHER; DESERTS.)

Engelmann's Pear

Pincushion Cactus

Barrel Cactus

Organ Pipe Cactus

Saguaro or Giant Cactus

Night-blooming Cereus

The head of Augustus Caesar on a coin.

Julius Caesar led the Roman legions in wars of conquest.

CAESARS (SEE zers) The Caesars were rulers of ancient Rome. The words "czar" and "kaiser" both came from the word "Caesar." "Caesar" was at first the last name of a famous ruler, Julius Caesar. Then it became a title that meant "emperor."

Julius Caesar was a great warrior. He conquered all the part of Europe that is now France. He even marched his armies into Britain. He also took them to the east and conquered part of Asia.

After one of his battles in Asia, Caesar sent back a famous message to Rome. It is famous because it told so much in so few words. The message was *Veni, vidi, vici.* Translated into English the message is, "I came, I saw, I conquered."

Julius Caesar was more than a good warrior. He brought about many changes that were good. For one thing he made a new calendar. It has come down to us almost as he made it. The month of July was named for him.

The month of August was named for another famous Caesar—Augustus. Augustus was the ruler of the great Roman Empire when Christ was born. It was an order of his that sent Joseph and Mary to Bethlehem. But Augustus did not have any idea that people in later centuries would think that the birth of Jesus was the most important happening in his reign.

The real name of Augustus was Octavius. The Romans gave him the name Augustus because they admired him so much. "Augustus" means "admired" or "revered." Some of his people even thought that he was a god.

Augustus was a good ruler. He ruled for 45 years. This long reign was one of the bright spots in the history of Rome.

There were other Caesars. Some were good. Some were bad. At least under them the Romans had peace and prosperity for two centuries. (See CALENDAR; ROME.)

Roman soldiers conquered the tribes of France.

CAISSON The foundations of many sky-scrapers and big bridges go deep into the earth till they reach solid rock. Many tunnels are built underground—some of them under rivers, lakes, or arms of the sea. One of the problems in sinking deep foundations and building tunnels is to keep water out. Even on dry land water is sure to come into a hole if it is dug deep enough.

In building foundations and tunnels, caissons are often used. The diagram shows a caisson being used in building a tunnel. In a caisson compressed air is used to keep water out.

The caisson itself is a big tube made of steel or concrete. At first it stands on end on the ground or on the floor of the river, lake, or sea. A few feet from the bottom there is an airtight ceiling called a deck. It makes the lower part of the caisson into a working room. To sink the caisson workmen inside it dig out the sand or soil underneath. The men who do this kind of work inside a caisson are called sandhogs.

To shut water out, compressed air is constantly pumped into the working room. This air would escape in a great hurry whenever a workman entered or left or a load of sand was lifted out if it were not "locked" in by means of an air lock. An air lock is a small room with two doors. One of them must always be closed.

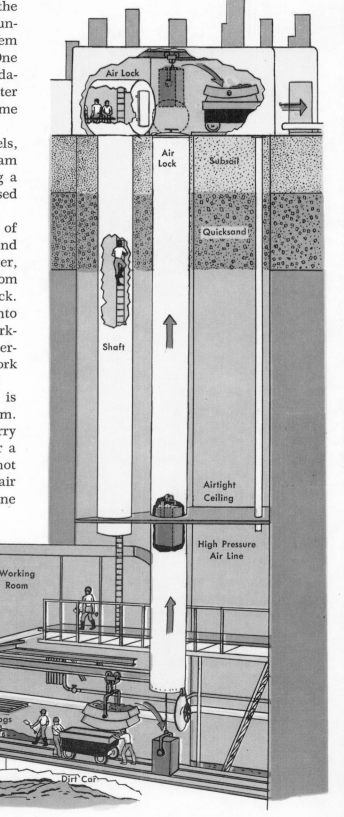

The air lock does more than lock air in the working room of the caisson. The air there is so compressed that it would be dangerous for the sandhogs to go into it or out of it quickly. As a sandhog goes to work, he stays in the air lock while air is gradually pumped in until the pressure is the same as in the working room below. As a sandhog leaves work, he stays in the air lock while the air is allowed to escape slowly until the pressure in the air lock is the same as that out of doors.

When, as in the picture, a caisson is used in building a tunnel, a barrel-shaped "shield" is pushed out through the wall of the caisson. It is pushed farther and farther ahead as the tunnel is dug.

When a caisson is used in building a foundation, it is often filled up with concrete as soon as it has been sunk down to bedrock. It then becomes a solid part of the foundation itself.

Work in a caisson is not easy. Only strong men can stand it. And once in a while there is an accident. Once, for instance, the compressed air burst out of the working room and blew a workman right up through a river.

CALCULATING MACHINES There are machines that can add and multiply and subtract and divide. They can do it much faster than a person can do it. And if they are in good order they do not make mistakes. These machines are called calculating machines.

Many offices have simple calculating machines called adding machines. An adding machine may be smaller than a typewriter.

But there are calculating machines that are as big as a big room. These machines—called "computers"—have many tubes much like radio tubes in them. The biggest computers are made of thousands and thousands of tubes. One machine can do in an hour problems that would take a person ten years to do with a pencil and paper.

But people still need to know how to add and subtract and multiply and divide. For calculating machines are not always available. Many of them, moreover, are expensive. The biggest cost more than a million dollars. Of course, no one would think of using one of these huge machines for the simple arithmetic problems most of us have. It would be as wasteful as using a cannon to kill a fly.

Office calculating machines are of many sizes and styles.

CALCUTTA India is one of the most crowded countries in the world. Calcutta, with its more than two and a half million people, is India's second-largest city.

This big city is on the delta of the Ganges, India's greatest river. The Ganges flows for more than a thousand miles across the plain of northern India. In places it is more than three miles wide. For century on century this big river has been bringing down sand and mud by the ton from the mountains to the west. The delta it has built up is many miles long and broad. The river now divides into several branches as it flows over the delta. Calcutta is on the branch called the Hooghly River.

Calcutta began about 250 years ago as a British trading post. The traders chose the spot partly because it was a little higher than the surrounding land. Much of the delta was flooded when the river was high. But in many ways the spot chosen is not a good place for a city. It is 80 miles from the sea. Ocean boats must come up the shallow Hooghly River. This river has to be dredged out often even though the tides help to scour it out. Much of the land around the city is swampy. In the summer the climate is almost unbearable. It is very hot and wet.

In spite of its handicaps, Calcutta grew fast. It is now one of the busiest ports in the world. It is the gateway to northern India. Goods from other lands go through Calcutta on their way to the millions of people of India. Most of the people of India are farmers. The jute, tea, and some of the other crops they raise go through Calcutta on their way to the rest of the world. Along the miles of docks in the city, boats are always being loaded and unloaded.

Calcutta has some factories. There are steel mills and sugar mills and jute mills. In no other place in the world is so much jute woven into burlap. There are shipbuilding yards, too.

Parts of Calcutta look much like American cities. There are well-paved streets lined with beautiful buildings. There are schools and museums and temples. There are big government buildings and homes large and splendid enough to be called palaces. There are parks and gardens. Automobiles and buses travel on the paved streets. But some streets of Calcutta are as crowded and dirty as any streets anywhere in the world. The poorest and most crowded streets are along the river. The people there live in mud huts. They are workers in the factories and on the docks. No one has to go any farther than this gateway city to know that India is a rich land that still has in it many poor people. (See BOMBAY; CITIES; DELTA; INDIA.)

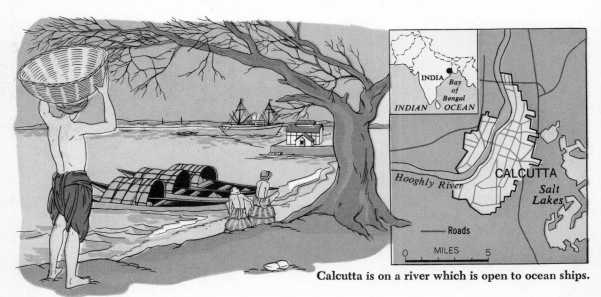

Calcutta is on a river which is open to ocean ships.

Early man used the moon in keeping track of time.

CALENDAR What day is today? When does Easter Sunday come this year? What day of the week will Christmas be? How long is it until vacation? To answer questions like these we look at a calendar.

A calendar looks very simple. But it took many centuries to work out our way of keeping track of time. The story of our calendar began back in the days before people could read or write.

Probably the first way of keeping track of time was to count days. Perhaps our early ancestors counted days by "suns." Some primitive peoples do now. Perhaps they kept track of the "darks" instead. Some primitive peoples still do. A day on our calendar is daytime and nighttime together. But not for a long, long time did people think of days like ours.

Almost as soon as people counted "suns" or "darks," they must have noticed the changes in the moon. The moon was full. Then it got smaller and smaller until it disappeared altogether. Then it grew into a full moon again. From full moon to full moon was a good measure of time. Our word "month" came from the word "moon."

In time, man saw that there were seasons which followed one another in regular order. In ancient Egypt the season when the Nile flooded the land was followed by the season when crops were planted and cared for. Then came the season of harvest. The circle of seasons became the year.

Our early ancestors did not know it, but the movements of the earth and the moon gave them their ways of keeping track of the time. The spinning of the earth makes the sun rise and set. The traveling of the moon around the earth makes the moon seem to change its shape. The traveling of the earth around the sun causes the circle of the seasons.

For a long time no one tried to fit days and months and years together. When they did, they ran into trouble. Days do not fit evenly into months. The time from full moon to full moon is about 29½ days. Days do not fit evenly into years. It takes the earth about 365¼ days to travel around the sun. And moon months do not fit evenly into years. The moon travels around the earth between 12 and 13 times in a year.

The priests of ancient Babylon worked out a calendar which had 29 days in some months and 30 days in others. Their year at first had 12 months in it. But it was several days too short. Soon the months had slipped out of place in the seasons. If every year of ours were several days shorter than the time it takes the earth to go around the sun, Christmas would soon come in the middle of our summer. To keep the months from slipping too far out of place in the seasons, the priests put an extra month in the year every two or three years.

Sundials were one of the first devices for telling time.

This ancient Chinese sphere was supposed to show the courses of the sun, moon, and planets.

The early Greeks had a calendar much like the Babylonian calendar. So did the early Romans. But in Rome politics began to have something to do with the calendar. Whenever the priests did not like someone who was elected to an office, they would make his term short by not putting an extra month in the year even if it was needed. On the other hand, they put in extra months, even when they were not needed, to make the terms of some officials longer.

When Julius Caesar became the ruler of the Roman Empire, the calendar was very badly mixed up. Caesar decided to throw out their moon-month calendar and start over. He asked some astronomers to help. For the new calendar they borrowed the idea of the year from the Egyptians. The Egyptians had worked out the length of

their year by watching the bright star Sirius. Their year began when Sirius appeared in the eastern sky at dawn, and was 365 days long.

Caesar's astronomers decided that a year should be 365¼ days long. They decided to have 365 days in a year for three years. Then every fourth year they would have a leap year with 366 days in it.

Since they had decided not to have true moon months, they could make the months any length they pleased. They chose to divide the year into 12 months of about the same length. It was easy to see that they could have five 31-day months and seven 30-day months. The Romans thought that odd numbers were lucky. To get an extra 31-day month, they took a day from a 30-day month—from February.

Julius Caesar named a month for himself—July. This month, of course, was given 31 days. When Augustus Caesar became emperor a few years later, the month after July was named for him. But it was only a 30-day month. A month named for an emperor could not have just 30 days! Another day, therefore, was taken from February to add a day to August. February was left with 28 days except in leap year.

Our months have come down to us unchanged from the time of Augustus Caesar. Our names for the months come from Ro-

Augustus Caesar

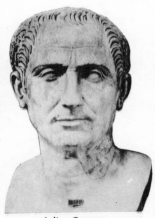

Julius Caesar

man names. Our weeks are like those in Caesar's calendar, too.

Caesar's plan of leap years was followed for about 1,600 years. But by that time dates had slipped a little out of place in the seasons. The trouble was that a year is not quite 365¼ days long. Caesar's calendar put in leap years too often. Pope Gregory decided to change the calendar to correct this mistake. In 1582 he asked an Italian astronomer to help him work out a better rule for leap years. We still follow his rule. It is: If a year's number can be divided by 4, it is a leap year unless it can be divided by 100. Even if it can be divided by 100, it is a leap year if it can be divided by 400.

To put the dates back in their proper places in the seasons, Pope Gregory moved the date up 10 days. October 5 of that year became October 15.

Some countries were very slow to accept the new calendar. The English-speaking countries did not use it until 1752. By that time the old calendar was so out of step

Hebrew Year 5720   Islamic Year 1378   Christian Year 1959

Aztec Calendar Stone

that the dates had to be moved up 11 days. Many people thought that they were losing 11 days out of their lives. There were great meetings at which the cry was, "Give us back our 11 days."

At the same time January 1 was made New Year's Day. Before that time March 25 had been the first day of the New Year.

We still use Pope Gregory's calendar. His rule for leap years works well. But some people think that our calendar should be changed. The World Calendar at the bottom of the page is one suggestion. It has been approved by several countries.

Present Calendar

FIRST QUARTER

JANUARY	FEBRUARY	MARCH
S M T W T F S	S M T W T F S	S M T W T F S
1	1 2 3 4 5	1 2 3 4 5
2 3 4 5 6 7 8	6 7 8 9 10 11 12	6 7 8 9 10 11 12
9 10 11 12 13 14 15	13 14 15 16 17 18 19	13 14 15 16 17 18 19
16 17 18 19 20 21 22	20 21 22 23 24 25 26	20 21 22 23 24 25 26
23 24 25 26 27 28 29	27 28	27 28 29 30 31
30 31		

SECOND QUARTER

APRIL	MAY	JUNE
S M T W T F S	S M T W T F S	S M T W T F S
1 2	1 2 3 4 5 6 7	1 2 3 4
3 4 5 6 7 8 9	8 9 10 11 12 13 14	5 6 7 8 9 10 11
10 11 12 13 14 15 16	15 16 17 18 19 20 21	12 13 14 15 16 17 18
17 18 19 20 21 22 23	22 23 24 25 26 27 28	19 20 21 22 23 24 25
24 25 26 27 28 29 30	29 30 31	26 27 28 29 30

THIRD QUARTER

JULY	AUGUST	SEPTEMBER
S M T W T F S	S M T W T F S	S M T W T F S
1 2	1 2 3 4 5 6	1 2 3
3 4 5 6 7 8 9	7 8 9 10 11 12 13	4 5 6 7 8 9 10
10 11 12 13 14 15 16	14 15 16 17 18 19 20	11 12 13 14 15 16 17
17 18 19 20 21 22 23	21 22 23 24 25 26 27	18 19 20 21 22 23 24
24 25 26 27 28 29 30	28 29 30 31	25 26 27 28 29 30
31		

FOURTH QUARTER

OCTOBER	NOVEMBER	DECEMBER
S M T W T F S	S M T W T F S	S M T W T F S
1	1 2 3 4 5	1 2 3
2 3 4 5 6 7 8	6 7 8 9 10 11 12	4 5 6 7 8 9 10
9 10 11 12 13 14 15	13 14 15 16 17 18 19	11 12 13 14 15 16 17
16 17 18 19 20 21 22	20 21 22 23 24 25 26	18 19 20 21 22 23 24
23 24 25 26 27 28 29	27 28 29 30	25 26 27 28 29 30 31
30 31		

Proposed World Calendar

FIRST QUARTER

JANUARY	FEBRUARY	MARCH
S M T W T F S	S M T W T F S	S M T W T F S
1 2 3 4 5 6 7	1 2 3 4	1 2
8 9 10 11 12 13 14	5 6 7 8 9 10 11	3 4 5 6 7 8 9
15 16 17 18 19 20 21	12 13 14 15 16 17 18	10 11 12 13 14 15 16
22 23 24 25 26 27 28	19 20 21 22 23 24 25	17 18 19 20 21 22 23
29 30 31	26 27 28 29 30	24 25 26 27 28 29 30

SECOND QUARTER

APRIL	MAY	JUNE
S M T W T F S	S M T W T F S	S M T W T F S
1 2 3 4 5 6 7	1 2 3 4	1 2
8 9 10 11 12 13 14	5 6 7 8 9 10 11	3 4 5 6 7 8 9
15 16 17 18 19 20 21	12 13 14 15 16 17 18	10 11 12 13 14 15 16
22 23 24 25 26 27 28	19 20 21 22 23 24 25	17 18 19 20 21 22 23
29 30 31	26 27 28 29 30	24 25 26 27 28 29 30 W

THIRD QUARTER

JULY	AUGUST	SEPTEMBER
S M T W T F S	S M T W T F S	S M T W T F S
1 2 3 4 5 6 7	1 2 3 4	1 2
8 9 10 11 12 13 14	5 6 7 8 9 10 11	3 4 5 6 7 8 9
15 16 17 18 19 20 21	12 13 14 15 16 17 18	10 11 12 13 14 15 16
22 23 24 25 26 27 28	19 20 21 22 23 24 25	17 18 19 20 21 22 23
29 30 31	26 27 28 29 30	24 25 26 27 28 29 30

FOURTH QUARTER

OCTOBER	NOVEMBER	DECEMBER
S M T W T F S	S M T W T F S	S M T W T F S
1 2 3 4 5 6 7	1 2 3 4	1 2
8 9 10 11 12 13 14	5 6 7 8 9 10 11	3 4 5 6 7 8 9
15 16 17 18 19 20 21	12 13 14 15 16 17 18	10 11 12 13 14 15 16
22 23 24 25 26 27 28	19 20 21 22 23 24 25	17 18 19 20 21 22 23
29 30 31	26 27 28 29 30	24 25 26 27 28 29 30 W

Worldsday (a World Holiday), W or 31 December (365th day), follows 30 December every year.
* The Leapyear Day (another World Holiday), W or 31 June, follows 30 June in leap years.

CALIFORNIA

OREGON

PACIFIC OCEAN

Eureka

Dyerville—"Founder's Tree" (Tallest Tree Known to Man—364 Feet High)

Redding

Eel River

Sacramento River

COAST

(F)

(F)

Sacramento

(F)

Golden Gate Bridge (4,200 Feet Long)

SAN FRANCISCO

San Mateo

Berkeley
Oakland
Alameda

San Jose

CENTRAL

(F)

(G)

Sutter's Sawmill (Gold Discovered, 1848)

Lake Tahoe

SIERRA

VALLEY

San Joaquin River

Merced

(F)

Fresno

NEVADA

(G)

Mount Whitney 14,495 Feet

Death Valley Nat'l. Monument (Lowest Point in the U.S., 282 Feet Below Sea Level)

RANGES

Bakersfield

(G)

(F)

Santa Barbara

Santa Monica

LOS ANGELES

Torrance
Long Beach

Burbank
Glendale

Pasadena

(F)

San Bernardino

Riverside

Anaheim (Disneyland)

Santa Ana

(F)

Mount Palomar (World's Largest Reflecting Telescope)

Salton Sea

San Diego

El Centro

Colorado River

ARIZONA

MEXICO

NEVADA

ELEVATION
Feet

| over 10000 |
| 7000 - 10000 |
| 5000 - 7000 |
| 3000 - 5000 |
| 2000 - 3000 |
| 1500 - 2000 |
| 1000 - 1500 |
| 600 - 1000 |
| 300 - 600 |
| 0 - 300 |
| Below sea level |

0   MILES   100

Legend

Oil	Fish
Aircraft	Cotton
Chemicals	Dairying
Garden Crops	Beef Cattle
Shipping	Lumbering
— Dams	(G) Grapes and Wine

(F) Fruit

Hardware

Machinery

Total state population . . . 13,922,000
Area (square miles) 158,693

▲ Historical Sites and Points of Interest

Mt. Wilson Observatory

Rocky Mountains

Oranges

Gold Rush Statue

State Flag

State Capitol Sacramento

Canning

Pears
Grapes

Lemons

Peppers

Movies

Grapefruit

THE GREAT SEAL OF THE STATE OF CALIFORNIA

EUREKA

State Flower
Golden Poppy

State Seal

CALIFORNIA This far Western state has a coast line stretching along the Pacific Ocean for more than 1,000 miles. In size California ranks third behind Alaska and Texas. In population, only New York is ahead of it. California has ten large cities of more than 100,000 people. Of these cities Los Angeles is the largest.

California was first a Spanish and then a Mexican colony. In 1848, Mexico ceded to the United States this region of ranches and Indian-Mexican villages. California became a state in 1850, the 37th to join the Union. The capital is Sacramento.

California has grown in population very rapidly. In 1848 gold was discovered there. The gold rush that followed in 1849 brought a flood of pioneers. Later, many of these pioneers took up farming. Wheat became California's "gold." Newcomers found the region very pleasant, with its mild climate, long seacoast, high mountains, green valleys, and desert scenery. They saw that there were many kinds of work to do in making use of its land, its forests, its minerals, and the ocean near its long coast.

Today California farmers and fishermen lead those of all other states in the dollar value of their products. The farmlands lie mainly in two regions, the Central Valley, or Great Valley, and southern California.

The Central Valley is about 450 miles long and 40 miles wide. It is bordered by the high Sierra Nevada Mountains on the east, and by the Coast Ranges on the west. Mountain streams are used to irrigate much of the land in the Valley. Central Valley farmers grow many kinds of crops, among them wheat and cotton. They keep dairy cows, sheep, and chickens, and fatten beef cattle that are brought down from mountain pastures.

In southern California, too, much of the farmland is irrigated. Farmers raise winter vegetables, oranges and other citrus fruits, dates, and cotton.

The most valuable of all California crops is cotton. Citrus fruits are second.

Factories and mills top the farmlands in dollars earned. Many factories prepare food, including fish, for market. Big mills make machinery, metal goods, and wood products. Near the coast in the southern part of the state there are rich oil wells and many refineries for making gasoline and other oil products.

The large cities of California are centers of manufacture and trade. Los Angeles is noted for oil refining and steelmaking. San Francisco, too, manufactures steel. San Diego and some other cities build airplanes. California leads all states in airplane construction. Hollywood, a part of Los Angeles, is the greatest motion-picture center in the world.

Until Alaska became a state in 1958, California's Mt. Whitney was the highest point in the United States. Now the highest point is Alaska's Mt. McKinley. But California still has the lowest land in the United States, Death Valley. There are four national parks in California. One of them has in it the only big stand of giant sequoias, or big trees. Among the man-made marvels in California are the Golden Gate Bridge, the great man-made harbor of San Pedro, the world's largest reflector telescope on Mt. Palomar, and old Spanish missions.

Oil

San Francisco-Oakland Bay Bridge

State Bird: California Quail

FOODS

This meal provides 1,034 calories.

CALORIE No one can live long without food. One reason why is that our bodies must have fuel. The foods we eat serve as fuel. They burn slowly in our bodies and furnish the heat and energy we need to keep us alive. The fuel value of a food is measured in calories. The word "calorie" comes from the Latin word meaning "heat."

Some foods furnish much more heat and energy than other foods do. The fuel value of a slice of watermelon, for instance, is only about 100 calories. But the fuel value of a piece of chocolate meringue (meh RANG) pie is about 450 calories.

Boys and girls use up so much energy that they need a great deal of fuel food. If they are from 9 to 12 years old, they need about 2,500 calories a day. If they do not get that many, some of their body fat burns up. If there is no fat, some of their body cells burn up instead.

Foods that furnish the most calories are not always the best for us. We must think not only of calories, but of other things, too, in choosing what we eat. (See FOODS.)

CALORIE CHART		
Food	Quantity	Calories
Apple	1 medium	75
Bacon	2 strips	100
Baked potato	1 medium	95
Carrots	1 cup	45
Chocolate milk	1 cup	185
Dried raisins	1 cup	430
Frankfurter	1	125
Jellybeans	6	50
Lettuce	2 leaves	5
Roasted peanuts	1 cup	805
Spinach	1 cup	45
Tangerine	1 small	35
Tomato	1 small	16
White bread	1 slice	65
Whole egg	1	75

CAMELS AND CARAVANS Camels live in hot desert lands. They are wonderfully fitted for life in regions where food and water are scarce.

These big animals can go for days without eating, because they store large amounts of food in their humps. When food is plentiful, they eat a great deal, much more than they need at the time. The extra food is stored in their humps as fat. How long a camel can go without eating depends on how quickly it uses up its stored food. If the camel is carrying a heavy load, it uses food fast. If it is not working as hard, the food lasts for a longer time.

Camels can also store enough water inside their bodies to last for three days or

Bactrian camels live in Asia.

even longer. When they come to a water hole, they drink a great deal. A thirsty camel has been known to drink 20 gallons of water at one time.

Camels are well fitted to stand the heat and the blowing sand of hot deserts. Soft pads protect their feet from the heat of the desert floor. The pads also keep their feet from sinking down into the sand. During sandstorms camels can close their nostrils to keep the sand out. Hairs keep the sand out of their ears, and long eyelashes keep it out of their eyes.

There are two kinds of camels. The Bactrian camel has two humps. Its home is in

Arabian camels live in Arabia and northern Africa.

central Asia. The Arabian camel has only one hump. This camel, found in Arabia and northern Africa, is sometimes called a dromedary. Some dromedaries are used for racing just as horses are.

Camels furnish meat and milk. They furnish hair that can be made into soft cloth. And they are a very important means of transportation in desert regions. Sometimes they are called "ships of the desert."

A camel can begin to carry heavy loads when it is 4 years old. It can continue until it is 25 or 30. As a rule a camel's load is about 400 pounds, but some camels can carry 1,000 pounds for short distances.

Long caravans of camels are a common sight on the deserts of Asia and Africa. These camel caravans move day and night, summer and winter. Of course, a caravan must stop now and then to give both the camels and their drivers a chance to rest.

In the Sahara regular bus and truck lines now operate across parts of the desert. In rough desert country, however, camels are still the best means of transportation. (See ADAPTATION TO ENVIRONMENT.)

Camels can endure the tremendous heat and sandstorms of the Sahara.

CAMEO Certain small carvings are called cameos. Cameos are used in rings and brooches. They were very popular for many centuries, but they are not so popular now.

To make a cameo, a sculptor must have a stone or shell with two layers of different colors. One must be light, the other dark. He carves figures in the light layer. Then he cuts away all the rest of that layer. The light carving now stands out against the darker background.

In earlier times similar carvings were used to decorate vases, bowls, and even furniture. The first cameos we know about were made in Greece over 2,000 years ago.

CAMERA There are wonderful pictures of Columbus, George Washington, Napoleon, and other famous men of earlier times. But these pictures are paintings, not photographs. Photographs became possible only a little more than 100 years ago after the camera was invented.

A camera is a light-tight box. Light can come into it only when a shutter is pulled away from a small opening at the front. Then the light shines in through a lens in the opening. The lens throws a picture of what is in front of it on a film or a plate at the back of the box. This film or plate is coated with a chemical sensitive to light.

Fortunately a camera lens can throw on a plate or film a small picture of a very large object. Otherwise, we could not take pictures of big buildings or clouds or crowds of people. After a picture is taken, the plate or film has to be developed.

A camera may cost only a few dollars or it may cost hundreds of dollars. One big difference between a cheap camera and an expensive one is in the quality of the lens. The best lenses are very expensive because they are very carefully ground.

Moving picture cameras are much like other cameras. They simply take one picture after another very rapidly. (See DAGUERREOTYPE; INVENTIONS; LENSES; MOTION PICTURES; PHOTOGRAPHY; TELEVISION.)

PARTS OF A CAMERA

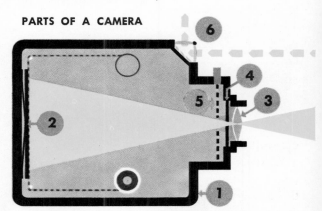

1. A camera is a specially made box that no stray light can get into.

2. The film is held in position at the back of the box. There is a winder to turn the film for another picture.

3. The lens is the eye of the camera. The better the lens, the better picture the camera can take.

4. The diaphragm has a hole that can be made larger or smaller. It can be set for just the right amount of light to take a good picture.

5. The shutter opens and closes very fast to snap the picture. Only when the shutter opens does light enter the camera.

6. The view finder shows the picture taker what his camera sees. With it he can aim the camera properly.

Miniature Camera

Studio Camera

Press Camera

Bellows Camera

CAMOUFLAGE (KAM o flazh) The spider crab has no good weapons for protecting itself. But it has a good way of hiding from its enemies. It plants tiny seaweeds and little animals of the sea on its back and on its long legs. They make it match its surroundings. When a spider crab travels to a new place it may change the plants and animals on its back.

The decorations of the spider crab are a kind of camouflage. Camouflaging anything means making it look so much like its surroundings that it is hard to see.

The animals in the picture do not have to camouflage themselves. They are naturally camouflaged. The tree hopper looks like a thorn. The walking stick and the measuring worm look like twigs. The tree toad matches the green leaf it is on. The viceroy butterfly and the monarch butterfly are hard at first glance to tell apart. The monarch is believed to have such a bad taste that birds do not eat it. A bird that has tasted a monarch is not likely to eat the viceroy, either.

There are many other examples of camouflage in nature. From all these examples people have learned a great deal about camouflage.

One of Shakespeare's plays, *Macbeth*, tells a story of camouflage. Macbeth thought that he could not be killed in battle because an old prophecy said that he could not be killed "Till Birnam forest come to Dunsinane." Macbeth, knowing that trees cannot walk, felt safe. But he was not. An enemy army marched through Birnam wood. To camouflage himself each soldier cut down a small tree and held it in front of him. The trees of Birnam wood really seemed to march to Dunsinane, and Macbeth was killed.

Camouflage is especially important in wartime. Most modern armies have camouflage experts.

In World War I many objects were painted to camouflage them. Artists worked out colors and patterns that could be used

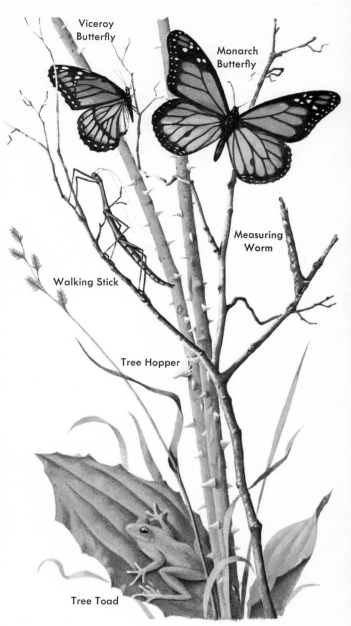

Viceroy Butterfly

Monarch Butterfly

Measuring Worm

Walking Stick

Tree Hopper

Tree Toad

to make an army truck or a boat or a gun seem to melt into its background. But in World War II camouflage was harder. Special filters were made for cameras so that an enemy, by taking pictures, could pick out objects painted to match the surroundings. Camouflage experts had to go back to the plan of the spider crab. They had to use real plants and sometimes even real animals rather than paint. (See PROTECTIVE COLORING.)

Asian nomads still live in tents.

CAMPING The only home that some people know even today is a tent. Most of us would not want to live in a tent for long. But every once in a while it is fun to go on a camping trip.

Living close to the outdoors is fun, especially for city people. But most people who go camping want something more than being out of doors. Some want to fish or to hunt. Some want to hike, ride horseback, swim, or go canoeing.

There are many camp sites where camping is made easy. Some campers, however, want to be entirely on their own. They may even want the feeling of really being in the wilderness.

Where shall we go, and how shall we get there? What clothing will we need? What food shall we take? What kind of tent shall

Indian tents were called tepees.

we have? What bedding and what cooking equipment will be best? What other equipment will we need? These are questions all campers must ask themselves.

Of course, the question of where to go is the first one to settle. The answer to it will help answer all the others. One good rule about clothing is that it should be comfortable and not easily torn. One good rule about food is that it should be the kinds that will not spoil readily.

Many new inventions make camping easier. There are boats that are very light in weight. There are tents that can be opened up like umbrellas, mattresses that can be blown up like balloons, and sleeping bags that make blankets unnecessary. And there are mess kits in which two kettles, a coffee pot, cups, plates, knives, forks, and spoons all fit together with a frying pan for a lid.

Campers always run some dangers. One danger is impure water. But water can be made safe by boiling it. There is also the danger of getting lost. A good camper always carries a compass. There is danger of accidents, too. No camper should be without a first-aid kit.

After a party of campers has reached the region they chose, there are many things to think about in picking out the exact camping spot. There should be water near, and there should be dry wood for a fire. There should be no poison ivy or poison sumac close by. The ground should be dry. The tent should be on a slope if possible so that rain water will drain off. If it is summer time, the tent should be where the breezes can reach it. It should not be under a single tall tree, because lightning might strike the tree in a thunderstorm. Of course, campers should get any permission needed to set up camp.

Campers can show they are good citizens by leaving their camping place in good shape. Most important, the campfire should be put out. Many forest fires have been caused by careless campers.

The boys in the picture have chosen a good place for camping. They have a proper campfire a safe distance from their tent. And each camper is doing a share of the work. To make camping a success, the campers must work together and must follow any rules that have been made for running the camp.

CANADA Of all the countries in the world, only the Soviet Union and China are larger than Canada. It has nearly a million square miles more than the continent of Australia, and over half a million more than the United States.

Over 3,000 miles of border separate Canada and the United States. This long border is not fortified in any way. Canada and the United States have shown the world how peaceably neighbor nations can live together.

Even though Canada is bigger than the United States, it does not have nearly as many people in it. It does not have a tenth as many.

Its climate helps explain why there are so few people in so big a land. The northern part of Canada has very long, cold winters. It is Eskimo land. Over most of the rest of Canada the winters are longer and colder than in the United States. Only in the southern part and on the west coast is the climate as mild as in the middle-western part of the United States.

A trick played by the glaciers of the great Ice Age is another reason for Canada's small population. During the Ice Age all of Canada—of course it was not Canada then—was covered time after time with great sheets of ice. These ice sheets moved southward into what is now the United States. As they did so, they scraped up soil from Canada and pushed it down into the United States. They left it there when they melted away. Now much of Canada's soil is thin and rather poor.

Parts of Canada were first settled by the French, parts of it by the English. In eastern Canada visitors see many signs in French, such as *Frais oeufs* and *Arrêtez, regardez, écoutez. Frais oeufs* means "Fresh eggs," and *Arrêtez, regardez, écoutez* means "Stop, look, listen."

Quebec is the most French of Canada's big cities. In Canada's largest city, Montreal, there is a mixture of French and English. Many signs are in both languages.

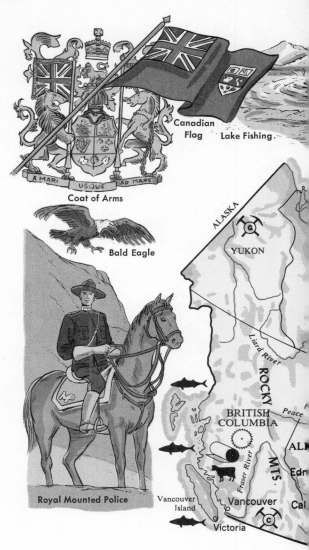

Canadian Flag · Lake Fishing

Coat of Arms

Bald Eagle

Royal Mounted Police

ALASKA

YUKON

Liard River

ROCKY

BRITISH COLUMBIA

Peace

Fraser River

MTS.

Edn

Cal

Vancouver Island

Vancouver

Victoria

Canada belongs to the British Commonwealth of Nations. The country rules itself very much as the United States does. But the people of Canada accept the king or queen of England as their sovereign.

Canada's capital is Ottawa. The country is divided into provinces much as the United States is divided into states. Each province has its capital. There are fewer provinces in Canada than there are states in the United States, but many of the provinces are very large.

Furs, farms, forests, and fisheries make up much of Canada's wealth. But the country is also rich in some minerals. The largest asbestos mines in the world are in the

province of Quebec. The largest nickel mines in the world are in the province of Ontario. Besides, Canada has copper, zinc, lead, silver, gold, and uranium. Compared with the United States, Canada is poor in coal and petroleum.

Mining goes on chiefly in the eastern provinces. Trapping goes on chiefly in the north. Furs from the Hudson Bay region were famous as far back as 200 years ago.

There are fisheries along both the east and the west coasts. South of Newfoundland is one of the greatest fishing regions in the world.

Much of the northeastern part of Canada is covered with forests. A great deal of the wood is used for making paper. The newspapers of the United States would have a hard time getting all the paper they need if it were not for Canada's forests.

The farms of eastern Canada are rather small. Potatoes are an important crop. Near the Great Lakes there are many orchards.

Stretching west from the Great Lakes and Hudson Bay there are great prairies. The farms here are big. Spring wheat is the chief crop. Big herds of cattle graze on the prairie grasses. Grain elevators and cattle pens are common sights. Winnipeg is the chief city of the prairie provinces.

West of the prairies there is a mountain wonderland. The Canadian Rockies are higher than the Rockies in the United States. The scenery is beautiful. Lake Louise, one of the mountain lakes, is famous for its beauty. Tourists from many parts of the world flock there in summer.

British Columbia is on the Pacific coast. Its climate is much like the climate of southern England. It has orchards, fisheries, forests of conifers, and lumber mills.

More than three-fourths of all the manufacturing that goes on in Canada is carried on in the provinces of Quebec and Ontario, much of it in the cities of Montreal and Toronto. It is partly because of its factories that Montreal is Canada's biggest city. Toronto is next in size.

It is easy for Canada to send its products abroad. Nova Scotia stretches far out into the Atlantic. It has been called Canada's "long wharf." Ocean boats travel up the St. Lawrence River to Montreal. The new St. Lawrence waterway will make Toronto an inland seaport. Vancouver in British Columbia is a good port on the Pacific.

Most of what Canada has to sell to other lands is bulky. Much of it is carried on its way to the ports by water. There are many lakes, rivers, and canals. There are good roads and railroads, too. The Canadian Pacific Railway stretches across the country.

Canada has made a name for itself for keeping law and order among its people. The Royal Canadian Mounted Police are famous all over the world.

Canada has a bright future. It has minerals that are not yet being mined. It has farmland that is not yet being farmed. It still has vast forests. Above all, its people are energetic. They are eager to keep Canada a great country. (See ARCTIC REGIONS; BRITISH EMPIRE; MONTREAL; NEWFOUNDLAND; QUEBEC; ST. LAWRENCE RIVER; YUKON.)

Shipping moves on the St. Lawrence Seaway.

Cattle raising is becoming more and more important in Canada. Farms in the great prairie region of Canada average 300 acres. Many are 1,500 acres or more. Much modern farm machinery is being used.

There are many thousands of square miles of forests in Quebec. Much of the wood from these forests is made into paper for newspapers in the United States. Canada gets about $500,000,000 for its newsprint.

Many of the paper mills are along the St. Lawrence River. After the logs are cut, they are floated down smaller streams to the St. Lawrence, and then down to the mills. Sometimes boats called "alligators" tow great "booms" of logs.

Many of the French-Canadians in the province of Quebec live almost as simply as the early settlers. They do not care for the busy life of big cities. They prefer to keep the language and traditions of their forefathers.

The fishing industry gives work to many thousands of people in Canada. Lobster and cod are caught in the Atlantic Ocean off Canada. Salmon and halibut come from the Pacific. Rivers and lakes yield whitefish and lake trout.

The Erie Canal is famous in songs and stories.

CANALS A canal is a man-made waterway. Some canals are built as highways for ships. Some carry water to irrigate desert land. Some are drainage canals. The world's biggest and longest canals are for ships.

A ship canal may be a short cut between two big bodies of water. It may be built beside a river that has rapids or falls in it which boats cannot pass. It may be built from a lake or sea to an inland city which has no river near it.

The idea of canals is not new. Nearly 4,000 years ago the Egyptians built a ship canal that joined the Nile with the Red Sea. Parts of this canal are still in use. Another old canal still in use is the Grand Canal in China. It was built about 700 years ago in the reign of the famous Kublai Khan. This canal is 1,000 miles long.

The Erie Canal was one of the early, important canals in the United States. It ran from Lake Erie to the Hudson River. DeWitt Clinton was the Governor of New York when it was built in 1825. People made fun of the canal while it was being dug. They called it "Clinton's Ditch." But it was soon a busy highway. Not long after it opened, as many as 50 boats a day were leaving Albany to travel westward through it. It had much to do with the spread of our country to the West. This canal is now a part of the New York State Barge Canal.

Some ship canals go uphill. If they do, they must have locks. There have to be locks, for instance, in the Soo Canals. These canals join Lake Superior and Lake Huron. The level of the water in Lake Huron is lower than the level of the water in Lake Superior.

Gondolas are taxis on the Grand Canal in Venice.

A lock is a kind of elevator. It is a section of a canal that has a watertight gate at each end. The water above the lock is several feet higher than the water below it. Suppose a boat is going upstream. It comes to the lower gate of the lock. The gate opens and the boat moves in. The gate closes behind it. Then water pours into the lock. As soon as the water in the lock is as high as the water above it, the upper gate opens and the boat moves into the upper level of

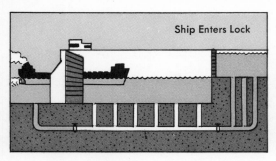

Ship Enters Lock

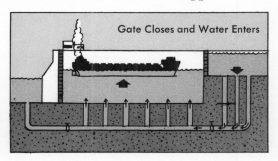

Gate Closes and Water Enters

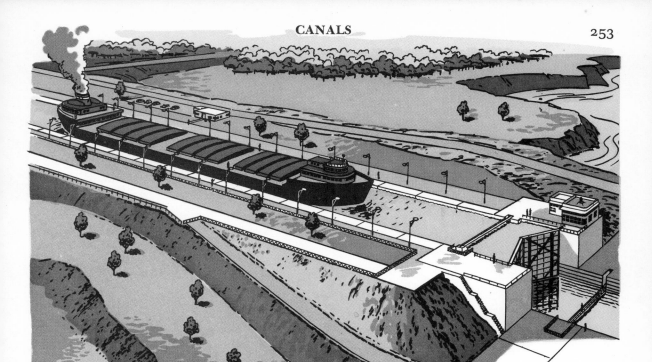

The Grasse River Lock of the new St. Lawrence Seaway raises or lowers ships 45 feet.

the canal. In some cases the whole lock moves up like the elevator in a building and lifts the boat up to the next level.

Boats must not go fast through canals, even if there are no locks. The waves they stir up when they go fast could do too much damage to the banks. In many canals, boats are not allowed to go under their own power. Mules walking along the banks used to tow boats along. Even earlier, in Asia, men towed them. Now in most of the world's canals there are small tugboats or engines running along the shore for towing.

Two of the world's most important canals are the Panama Canal and the Suez Canal. The Panama Canal links the Atlantic and Pacific oceans. The Suez Canal links the Mediterranean Sea with the Red Sea. Much of the world's shipping goes through these two famous canals. (See PANAMA CANAL; SUEZ CANAL.)

Canal	Country	Length in Miles	Width in Feet
Albert	Belgium	82	56
Amsterdam-Rhine	Netherlands	45	210
Cape Cod	United States	8	500
Corinth	Greece	4	72
Göta	Sweden	56	47
Houston	United States	49	195
Kiel	Germany	61	146
Manchester	England	35.5	85
Panama	Canal Zone	50.7	300
Soo (Sault Ste. Marie)	United States	1.6	100
Suez	Egypt	103	197
Welland	Canada	27.6	200

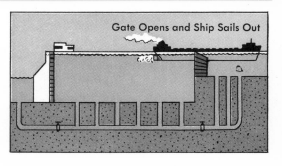

Ship Is Raised to Upper Level

Gate Opens and Ship Sails Out

Canaries are members of the finch family.

CANARY No cage birds are more popular than canaries. They are named for the Canary Islands, the home of their wild ancestors. There are still wild canaries on these islands.

Canaries became cage birds more than 400 years ago. They were taken from their home islands to many other parts of the world. People liked them as pets because they were good singers. Today there are about 50 varieties of canaries. The picture shows four of the many kinds.

Canaries raised in the Harz Mountains in Germany became famous long ago as good singers. Great care is taken in training them. They are really given singing lessons. Music is played for them. Besides, the young birds are kept with older birds that sing especially well.

A mother canary lays four or five blue eggs. The father bird does not help sit on them, but he helps with the feeding of the baby birds that hatch.

Canaries are not short-lived pets. Many live to be 15 or 16 years old. (See PETS.)

CANCER The tiny "bricks" our bodies are built of are called cells. A single one of these cells is too small to be seen without a microscope. Once in a while some cells somewhere in a person's body go on a rampage. They begin to grow and multiply very fast. In time they begin crowding other cells and stealing food the other cells need. They cause the disease which is called cancer.

Cancer used to be incurable. But now many people who have cancer get well. If it is discovered in time, the chances of curing it are very good. One reason why everyone should go to a doctor for a yearly checkup is to make sure no cancer cells are starting to grow.

Many doctors are at work in hospitals, universities, and laboratories trying to learn what causes cancer. When the cause is known, doctors will be better able to prevent and cure cancer. (See CELLS.)

CANDLES For a long, long time candles were the best way people had of lighting their houses after dark. Candles were much better than the smoky lamps and torches that went before them. Even now we use candles when we want soft light. We use many candles in churches, too.

No one knows who invented candles. Probably it was some monk of the Middle Ages who first made a candle like those we use now. Perhaps it happened in some such way as this:

A monk had a bowl of melted tallow. Tallow is the fat of sheep or oxen. He was dipping some small torches in the melted tallow so that they would burn more brightly. Beside the bowl lay the wick of one of the dish-shaped oil lamps of that time. By accident the monk spilled some tallow on the wick. The tallow soon hardened. When he lifted the wick up it was stiff. He lighted one end, and it burned with a bright little flame. "If there were more tallow around it," he thought, "it would last longer." He tried dipping it in tallow again and again. At last there was a thick layer of tallow around it, and it was stiff enough to stand up in a holder. He had made the first modern candle.

This story may be all wrong. But at least the first dipped candles we know about were candles made of tallow.

We still use many dipped candles, but most of them are made of wax instead of tallow. The wax is paraffin. In many cases it has been made a beautiful color.

Dipping candles is rather slow. Making candles in molds is much faster. In making candles in molds, the wicks are fastened in place first. Then the molds are simply filled with melted tallow or wax.

Molded candles are now made in many fancy shapes. At Christmas-time thousands and thousands of snowball, Christmas tree, angel, and Santa Claus candles are sold.

The wick is a very important part of a candle. When the wick starts to burn, it sets a little gas factory working. The heat of the burning wick melts some of the wax at the top of the candle. This wax soaks up the wick. When it reaches the center of the flame, it gets so hot that it turns to a gas. The gas moves outward in the flame and burns. Without a wick a candle would be very hard to light, and it would burn with an uneven, smoky flame. (See LAMPS AND LIGHTING.)

American settlers dipped their own candles by hand.

Candle Snuffers

Children ate honey cake
in the Middle Ages.

The Spaniards made sweetened
chocolate for centuries.

In the early days only the
rich could afford candy.

CANDY For many hundreds of years candy of a kind has been known. Long ago dates, figs, and nuts were chopped up, mixed with honey, and molded into pieces. But candy of the kinds we know—candy made of sugar—is much newer. Almost no one in Europe had ever heard of sugar until about 500 years ago, and it was very scarce for 200 years after that. Candy-making did not become common till sugar was plentiful.

A century ago doctors and druggists made candy for coatings on bad-tasting pills. Then people began making candy just for the taste of the candy. They invented many different kinds. Molasses taffy, licorice sticks, rock candy, and sugar plums are old-fashioned kinds of candy. Sugar plums were not plums. They were creamy candy made in the shape of plums.

All the candies of today are made chiefly of sugar. Some have gelatin or corn syrup in them. Some have nuts and fruits added.

At first all candy was made by hand. But now much candy is made by machine. There are many big candy factories. Of course, some is still made by hand at home.

A great deal of our candy of today is chocolate candy. Almost everyone likes the flavor of chocolate. Chocolate fudge is probably the commonest homemade candy.

Americans eat more candy than any other people in the world. The average is nearly 20 pounds of candy a person a year! (See CHOCOLATE AND COCOA; SUGAR.)

Too eager children have spilled many
a plate of sticky homemade candy.

Chinese children love
red candied apples.

Skull-shaped candy is a favorite
with the children of Mexico.

There are few tribes of cannibals today.

CANNIBALS Most people shudder at the thought of eating other people. Even among savages the custom of eating human flesh is rare today. Probably nowhere except on certain Pacific islands are there any people who are still cannibals.

Eating human flesh used to be rather common. In fact, some civilized peoples were cannibals. When the Spaniards conquered Mexico 400 years ago, they were horrified to find that the highly civilized Aztecs ate the flesh of some of the warriors they captured in battle.

Different cannibal groups probably became cannibals for different reasons. Some believed that eating brave warriors would make them brave themselves. To others cannibalism was a part of their religion. Some probably became cannibals simply because it was hard for them to get enough to eat. In parts of the world where living was difficult it became the custom in some tribes to kill and eat old people. It was a sign of lack of respect not to do so. Possibly many primitive peoples would still

eat human flesh if they had not been forced by outsiders to stop doing so.

Cannibalism is rather common among some kinds of animals. Many fishes, for example, eat some of the tiny fish that hatch from their own eggs.

Even some baby animals are cannibals. Baby garden spiders hatch from eggs enclosed in a silken sac. They immediately begin eating one another up. Only a few spiders come out of the sac. They have all the others inside them. (See SAVAGES.)

CAPE A cape is an arm of land that reaches out into a lake or a sea. There is no difference between a cape and a peninsula except that a peninsula is bigger.

Cape Ann, Cape Fear, Cape May, and Cape Hatteras are famous capes in the United States. Cape Cod is a peninsula.

Small capes are often called points. There are a great many points along the Atlantic Ocean and the shores of the Great Lakes. (See CAPE HORN; CAPE OF GOOD HOPE; PENINSULA.)

CAPE HORN Cape Horn is the southern-most tip of South America. It is not actually on the continent itself. Instead, it is on one of the many islands that hug the coast.

On the Cape steep slopes rise from the sea. There are many storms along the shore, so many that sailors used to boast of having safely "rounded the Horn."

The Cape was discovered in 1616 by a Dutch explorer, who came from a village named Hoorn. He named the Cape after this village. Later its name was shortened from Hoorn to Horn.

The route around Cape Horn joins the Atlantic and the Pacific. It is not as important a route as it once was. Most boats on their way from one ocean to the other now go through the Panama Canal.

CAPE OF GOOD HOPE A few years before Columbus discovered America, a Portuguese explorer set out on a voyage along the west coast of Africa. The explorer was Bartholomeu Dias. Dias sailed until he came to the southern end of Africa. He saw that it was possible to sail around the tip. The discovery was good news, for in those days explorers were hunting for an all-water route to India. They wanted an easy way of bringing back silks and spices from the East.

Dias went back to Portugal to report his discovery to the king. He gave the king a map he had drawn of Africa. The map showed a cape at the southern end of the west coast. Dias had named it the Cape of Storms because he had run into terrible storms there. The king was much pleased at the idea of a new route to India. He suggested that the cape be called the Cape of Good Hope. It has had this name ever since, but its name is often shortened to simply "the Cape."

There is a queer, flat-topped mountain on the Cape. It is called Table Mountain. Over the mountain there is often a cloud which looks a little like a white tablecloth.

The Cape of Good Hope is not the very southernmost point in Africa. Cape Agul-has, more than a hundred miles to the east, extends a little farther south.

Ten years after Dias made his discovery, another Portuguese explorer, Vasco da Gama, sailed around the tip of Africa and on to India. The route around the Cape was a very important one until the Suez Canal furnished a shorter way to the Far East. (See EXPLORERS; SUEZ CANAL.)

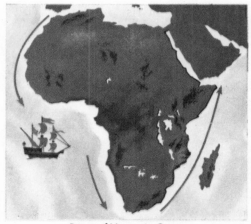

Route of Vasco da Gama

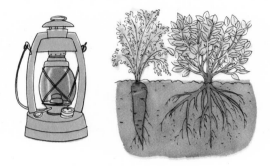

Towels, plant roots, and lamp wicks can do their jobs only because of capillary attraction, which makes liquids seem to defy gravity.

CAPILLARY ATTRACTION If a small glass tube is stood up in a glass of water, water will rise in the tube past the level of the water in the glass. The water is pulled up by the walls of the tube. Scientists call this pull "capillary attraction."

Water is pulled into the tiny spaces between the threads of a towel by capillary attraction. If it weren't for capillary attraction, a towel would be no better than a piece of oilcloth for drying one's hands.

If it weren't for capillary attraction, a blotter would not blot up ink. Paraffin would not soak up into a candlewick. Oil would not rise in the wick of an oil lamp. Most important of all, water deep in the ground would not rise through the soil to the roots of plants. If capillary attraction should stop, most of the plants in the world would soon be dead.

CARBON Out of all the chemical elements—the materials the world is built of —carbon is one of the most important. An entire branch of chemistry deals with the thousands of compounds of carbon.

There could not be any living things without carbon. For carbon makes up a part of the living material in every plant and animal. We ourselves are part carbon.

Carbon is also a part of all our common fuels. Wood, coal, coke, charcoal, fuel oil, gasoline, and cooking gas all have some carbon in them.

Almost all our foods contain carbon. In fact, salt and water are the only things we eat or drink that are not part carbon. Carbon is in many other substances, too.

Soot and coke and charcoal are almost pure carbon. From them one would guess that pure carbon is black. Sometimes it is, but not always. The "lead" in our lead pencils is not really lead. Instead it is a form of carbon called graphite. Graphite is iron-gray with a metal-like shine. More surprising, carbon can be clear and sparkling. For diamonds are carbon!

Vinegar, vaseline, and silk all have carbon in them. But how different they look! And not one of them looks at all like diamonds or graphite or soot. In many of the materials that have carbon in them, the carbon is joined with other elements to form compounds. In a compound an element may be very well hidden. Once in a while the carbon in a compound comes out of hiding. Suppose someone is making candy and lets it burn. The black stuff left in the pan is the carbon that was once a well-hidden part of the sugar. (See COAL; DIAMONDS; SUGAR.)

CARBON AS GRAPHITE

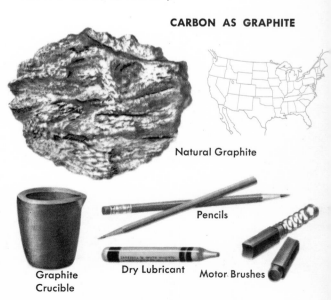

Natural Graphite

Pencils

Graphite Crucible

Dry Lubricant

Motor Brushes

Carbon dioxide in breath turns limewater milky.

CARBON DIOXIDE When ginger ale is poured into a glass, it foams. The same thing happens with all kinds of soda drinks. Ice-cream sodas foam, too. The foam on all these drinks is made of tiny bubbles of carbon dioxide. The carbon dioxide helps to make the drinks refreshing.

CO_2 is the chemist's way of writing carbon dioxide. The C stands for carbon, and the O for oxygen. The chemist's way of writing the name shows that in carbon dioxide there are two atoms of oxygen for every atom of carbon.

Carbon dioxide is produced in many ways. Almost all fires give off carbon dioxide. It can be made by mixing baking soda and vinegar. It can be made by adding water to baking powder. Yeast produces bubbles of carbon dioxide when it is put in bread dough. We ourselves breathe out carbon dioxide all the time. It comes from the slow "burning" of the food we eat. All

Fires give off carbon dioxide.

other animals breathe out carbon dioxide just as we do. No wonder there is always some carbon dioxide in the air!

Carbon dioxide is a very important substance. It does far more than make sodas taste good and make bread and cake puff up. Many fire extinguishers work by producing carbon dioxide. More important, green plants use carbon dioxide in making sugar. Without carbon dioxide for making sugar, they could not live. Neither could we, for we can trace all our food except salt and water back to the sugar that is manufactured by green plants.

Carbon dioxide is a gas. But it can be frozen so that it is as solid as a rock. We call frozen carbon dioxide "dry ice." Dry ice is so cold that it is dangerous to handle. It is useful in packing ice cream and other frozen foods for shipping. Unlike real ice, it does not make anything wet. Instead of melting, dry ice changes back to a gas. (See AIR; BREAD; PLANT FACTORIES.)

CARBON MONOXIDE When carbon burns in air that has little oxygen in it, the gas carbon monoxide is formed. It is formed, for instance, when the engine of an automobile runs in a closed garage.

In carbon monoxide there is only one atom of oxygen for every atom of carbon. The chemist's formula for it is CO. It will grab up more oxygen whenever it has a chance. Many people have died from breathing carbon monoxide. The gas is very poisonous because it keeps the blood from carrying oxygen.

But this dangerous gas can be useful, too. It can be used to take oxygen from places where it is not wanted. Most iron ore, for example, has oxygen in it. Carbon monoxide can be used to take the oxygen from the ore and leave only the iron.

CARBORUNDUM Diamonds are harder than anything else in the world. But crystals of carborundum are almost as hard. "Carborundum" is a trade name. Scientists call carborundum "silicon carbide."

Diamonds are dug out of the ground. Carborundum crystals have to be made. Carborundum was invented accidentally in 1891 by Edward Goodrich Acheson. The inventor was trying to make diamonds.

Today carborundum crystals are made in electric furnaces out of a mixture of sand and coke. The mixture is heated very, very hot. The temperature inside the furnace has to be more than 3,500° F. to make the crystals form.

Near Niagara Falls there is a big plant for making carborundum. Electricity for the furnaces comes from a power plant in which the generators are driven by water power. Operating the furnaces costs less than if the current came from generators driven by steam engines.

Carborundum is useful for grinding and polishing other hard materials. It is crushed into fine grains before it is used. Sometimes solid wheels and other tools for grinding and polishing are made of it. The pictures show some of the other uses of this very hard material.

Power for Making Carborundum

First Furnace

Edward G. Acheson
Inventor of Carborundum

Modern Furnace

USES OF CARBORUNDUM

Grinding Small Bearings

Rocket Engine Linings

Resistors

Sandpaper

Industrial Grinding

Sanding Belts

Grinding Wheels

Dental Drills

CARDS, PLAYING Hundreds of different games can be played with playing cards. Playing cards come in decks of 52 suit cards and, as a rule, one or two jokers.

Cards came to the United States from Europe. They came to Europe from the East. Perhaps the Moors brought them into Spain. Perhaps knights coming home from the Crusades brought them. At any rate they reached Europe sometime in the Middle Ages. We know they were used in Italy in 1279. Long before then they were common in China and India.

Decks of cards have not always looked like those we have now. Some cards were square. Some were much narrower than ours. Some were even round. The idea of marking them with diamonds, hearts, clubs, and spades came from France. Early German cards had acorns, bells, hearts, and leaves. Early Spanish cards were marked with swords, batons, cups, and money. Each suit has not always had a king, a queen, and a jack. Suits once had knights instead of queens. Some decks had extra cards which were used to foretell the future.

The first cards were made by hand. Some were beautifully gilded and painted. Of course, they were expensive. A French king once paid $500 for three decks.

Today cards are made by machines. They go from machine to machine until they are ready to be sold. They start their trip at a big printing press. All the cards for two decks are printed on a big sheet of cardboard. This big sheet goes to another machine where the cards are cut out and piled into decks. The magical fingers of still other machines gild the edges of the decks, wrap them in cellophane, and put them in boxes. Cards are now cheap enough so that almost everyone can have them.

CARIBBEAN SEA In the days when pirates were the terror of the seas, the Caribbean Sea was one of their favorite hunting grounds. In inlets along its shores pirates lay in wait to attack ships full of treasure sailing away from the lands that were then called the Spanish Main.

Pirates roamed the Caribbean.

The Caribbean is an arm of the Atlantic Ocean. As the map shows, the east coast of Central America, the north coast of South America, and the islands of the West Indies form its borders. Sometimes this sea is called the American Mediterranean.

The Caribbean is an important highway. It swarms with ships carrying coffee and bananas and oil from lands along its shores. Besides, all the ships that go through the Panama Canal must pass through it. Many

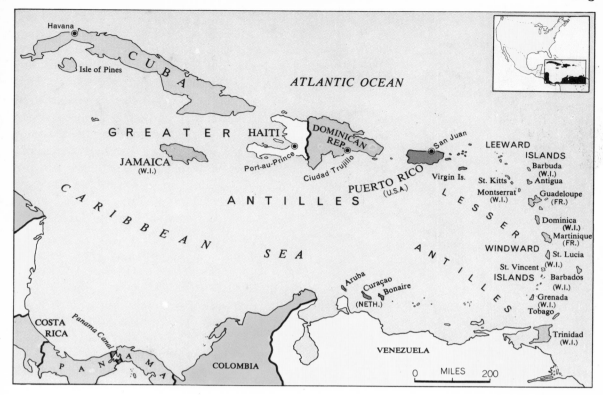

Havana

CUBA

Isle of Pines

ATLANTIC OCEAN

GREATER

HAITI

DOMINICAN REP.

JAMAICA (W.I.)

Port-au-Prince

Ciudad Trujillo

San Juan

LEEWARD

ISLANDS

Barbuda (W.I.)

Antigua

PUERTO RICO (U.S.A.)

Virgin Is.

St. Kitts

Montserrat (W.I.)

Guadeloupe (FR.)

ANTILLES

LESSER

Dominica (W.I.)

Martinique (FR.)

WINDWARD

St. Lucia (W.I.)

St. Vincent (W.I.)

ISLANDS

Barbados (W.I.)

Grenada (W.I.)

Tobago

CARIBBEAN

SEA

ANTILLES

Aruba

Curaçao

Bonaire

(NETH.)

COSTA RICA

Panama Canal

PANAMA

COLOMBIA

VENEZUELA

Trinidad (W.I.)

0   MILES   200

pleasure boats travel on the Caribbean, too. A cruise on this southern sea makes a pleasant winter vacation.

There are no longer any pirates in the Caribbean. But there are still dangers there. Hurricanes sometimes sweep in from the Atlantic and do much damage. Mountains under the sea are another danger. Some of their tops form islands. But some of the tops are just under the surface of the sea. Ship captains must be careful not to run aground on them. (See CENTRAL AMERICA; CUBA; PIRATES; PUERTO RICO; WEST INDIES.)

FISHES OF THE CARIBBEAN

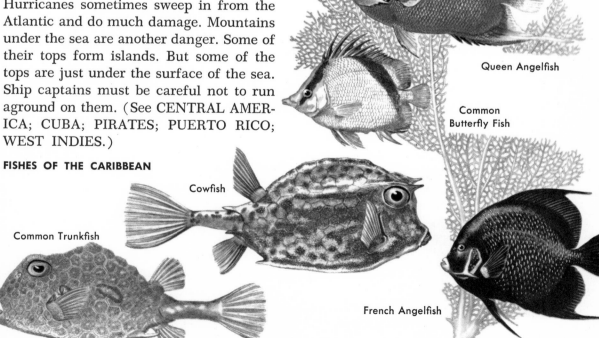

Queen Angelfish

Common Butterfly Fish

Cowfish

Common Trunkfish

French Angelfish

FAMILY TREE OF CARNIVORES

Dogs

Weasels

Foxes

Badgers

Civets

Bears

Hyenas

Raccoons

Cats

CARNIVOROUS ANIMALS A carnivorous animal is one that lives entirely, or almost entirely, on meat. "Carnivorous" means "meat eating."

Probably the meat eater we know best is the dog. Foxes, wolves, and all the other members of the dog family are meat eaters, too. So are lions, tigers, and all the other members of the cat family.

These meat eaters belong to a group of mammals called carnivores. The chart shows several other carnivores.

Moles are mammals and they are carnivorous, but they do not belong to the carnivores. They are called insectivores because they eat insects. Killer whales are among the fiercest of carnivorous mammals. They belong to a still different group, the cetaceans (see TA seeans).

Many birds are meat eaters. Hawks and owls catch many mice. Pelicans are among the birds that live mostly on fish. Woodpeckers, nuthatches, and swallows live chiefly on insects.

Most reptiles are meat eaters. Alligators and crocodiles are famous for their big mouths, strong jaws, and sharp teeth. Some snakes kill small animals to eat by squeezing them to death.

Toads and frogs are carnivorous for only a part of their lives. When they are tadpoles, they eat plants. When they grow up, they eat insects and worms.

Barracudas and sharks are carnivorous fishes. They eat mostly smaller fish. But they eat other animals, too, when they have a chance. Many fishes live on a fish diet. Some can eat fishes bigger than themselves.

Mammals, birds, reptiles, toads and frogs, and fishes are all backboned animals. There are many meat eaters among the animals without backbones, too.

Some of these backboneless meat eaters are insects. The praying mantis is such a greedy eater of other insects that it is sometimes called an insect tiger. The dragonfly, ladybug, giant water bug, and caterpillar hunter are a few of the other meat eating insects.

All spiders are carnivorous. Most of them spin webs that serve as insect traps.

Starfish eat oysters. The octopus eats crabs. Comb jellies live on tiny fish or shrimps. Centipedes eat soft-bodied in-

Carnivore's skull shows meat-tearing front teeth.

sects. The list of backboneless meat eaters could be made very long.

We eat meat, too. But we are not carnivorous, for we also eat plants. Most bears, even though they belong to the carnivores, eat some plant food. Animals which eat both plants and animals are called omnivorous. (See HERBIVOROUS ANIMALS; OMNIVOROUS ANIMALS.)

CARNIVOROUS PLANTS Everyone expects boys to eat apples. But no one expects apple trees to eat boys. They never do. But there are plants that eat animals. They are called carnivorous plants. These plants do not eat any very big animals. Most of the animals they eat are insects.

Of course, plants cannot go hunting. But each of the insect-eating plants has a way of its own of catching insects.

The leaves of a sundew plant act like flypaper. They are about half as big around as pennies. On them there are hairs, and on the ends of the hairs there are drops of sticky liquid. Insects get caught in the liquid. Their bodies are digested by it. The sundew gets its name because the drops of sticky liquid sparkle in the sun like dew.

Venus' flytrap has clever traps at the ends of its leaves. Each trap is a section of leaf that folds in the middle. On each half there are three signal hairs. For an insect to touch one of these hairs is like pulling a trigger. The trap closes at once, holding the insect fast. There is little chance that the insect will get away, because teeth around the edge of the trap lock together like the fingers of two hands. Digestive juices from the plant work on the trapped insect. When the soft parts of the insect are digested, the trap opens. What is left of the insect falls out and the trap is reset.

Pitcher plants also have traps. Their leaves are shaped like vases or pitchers. They catch and hold rain water. The vases are sweet smelling and brightly colored. Inside they have hairs that point downward. Attracted by the sweet smell and bright color, an insect lands on the edge of a pitcher and starts down into it. The hairs seem to say, "This way, please." But the wall is so slick that the insect soon slips into the rain water at the bottom.

Butterwort leaves are a combination of "flypaper" and traps. There are little openings all over the leaves. When an insect touches a leaf, a sticky liquid comes out of the openings. It holds the insect while the edges of the leaf curl up into a trap.

Carnivorous plants are not common. They are found only in places where some of the materials green plants need for food-making are scarce.

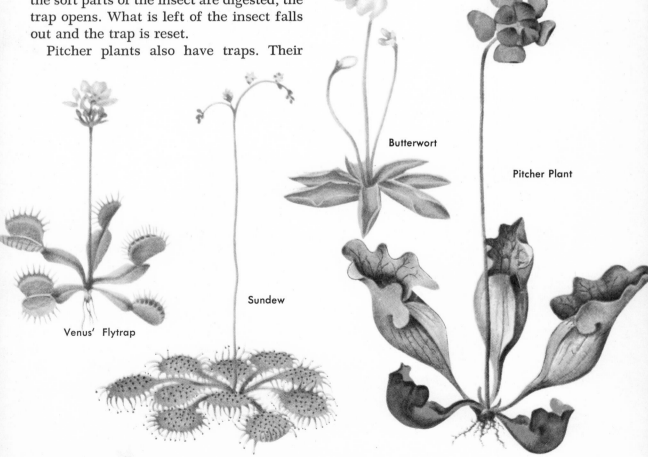

Venus' Flytrap

Sundew

Butterwort

Pitcher Plant

Navaho Weaving an Indian Rug

CARPETS AND RUGS The first rug was probably the skin of some animal. The first carpet—that is, the first floor covering that spread over the whole floor—was probably a layer of leaves or of straw. People of early times used these floor coverings because they were softer and warmer to bare feet than the hard floors of their caves and huts.

The weaving of floor coverings began more than 2,000 years ago. No one knows exactly when. No one knows exactly where, either. Probably it began in India or in some nearby part of Asia.

As far back as we can trace their story, rugs and carpets have been made on looms. The picture at the top of the page shows a rugmaker at her loom.

In making such a rug as she is making, long, strong threads are stretched up and down on the loom. They may be of cotton, wool, linen, jute, or some other fiber. These threads are called warp threads. Across

them other threads are woven in some fashion. These are the weft threads. The weft threads will show much more than the warp threads after the rug or carpet is finished. The weft threads are made of colored wool, cotton, silk, or rayon.

The first rugs were made by hand. The finest rugs are still handmade. For centuries the best have come from certain countries in Asia. They are called Oriental rugs. Tufts of threads of beautiful colors stand up from the base of an Oriental rug. They form the pile of the rug.

Oriental rugs are made in this way: The rugmaker arranges the warp threads on his loom. Then with beautifully colored yarns he ties a row of little knots, or tufts, across the warp threads. He next darns two weft threads in and out across the warp threads. He pushes these threads down against the row of tufts he has tied so that they will be held firm. He then ties another row of knots, and holds it in place with more weft threads. So he works until his rug is finished. He makes the design by choosing different colors for his knots.

In some of the finest Oriental rugs there are as many as 1,000 knots in one square inch. Usually there are not more than 400. But tying 400 knots in one square inch is slow and tedious. Some Oriental rugs have taken years to make.

The dyes the rugmakers use are the secret of the beauty of many Oriental rugs. Their dyes are made from plants or animals. One beautiful red color comes from sheep's blood. Many Oriental rugs have beautiful patterns, too. The patterns are handed down from generation to generation. Each family has its own pattern. The patterns have a great deal of meaning for the people of the countries where Oriental rugs are made.

Many of the people in the countries where Oriental rugs are made are Mohammedans. Mohammedans kneel to pray whenever, during the day, the call to prayer is sounded. A Mohammedan often has a small rug to kneel on. Some of the most beautiful rugs from the East are prayer rugs.

Today most rugs and carpets are made by machine. They are woven on big looms. Some of the looms can weave rugs and carpets 18 feet wide.

There are many types of machine-made rugs and carpets. The weaving of the pile yarns into the base is done in different ways. In some carpets and rugs the pile yarns stand up in loops. In others the loops are cut to make a smooth surface.

When an Oriental rugmaker makes the design in his rug, he has to choose the right color for every tuft. When a rug or carpet is woven on a power loom, the machine picks out the right color for each tuft or loop. The working of one of these big rug-making machines looks like magic.

MODERN RUG WEAVES

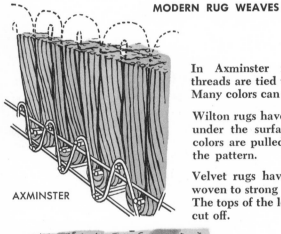

AXMINSTER

In Axminster rugs, raised threads are tied to a backing. Many colors can be used.

Wilton rugs have many yarns under the surface. Different colors are pulled up to make the pattern.

Velvet rugs have yarn loops woven to strong base threads. The tops of the loops are then cut off.

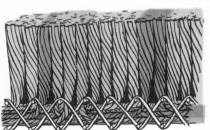

WILTON

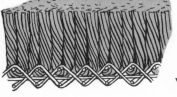

VELVET

An Ancient Persian Rug

CARROLL, LEWIS (1832-1898) The name signed to several famous nonsense stories for children is Lewis Carroll. But Lewis Carroll is only a pen name. The real name of the man who wrote the stories is Charles Lutwidge Dodgson. He was a professor of mathematics at Oxford University in England. Although Dodgson never married, he was always fond of children.

One summer he entertained the three young daughters of a friend by taking them for boat rides on the Thames (TEMS) River. One of the girls was named Alice. To amuse his guests, the professor began to tell a story of Alice's adventures in an underground world. All summer long he continued the story. The children loved it.

Later Dodgson made the story into a book. He printed it by hand and drew pictures in ink to illustrate it. He called it *Alice's Adventures Under Ground* and gave it to the real Alice.

In 1865 the book was published as *Alice's Adventures in Wonderland*. Children and grownups alike laughed at the Mad Hatter, the Dormouse, and the March Hare. The book was so popular that Dodgson wrote another one about Alice and her adventures. It was called *Through the Looking-Glass and What Alice Saw There*. The drawings for these two books when they were published were done by Sir John Tenniel. These drawings have become almost as famous as the stories themselves.

The original manuscript of *Alice in Wonderland,* which had been in the United States for many years, was taken back to England in 1948. Valued at $50,000, the manuscript is now in the British Museum. It was a gift to the British from a group of people in the United States.

Dodgson thought that his work as a teacher and writer on mathematics was more important than his nonsense writings. Almost no one today thinks of him as a great mathematician. He is far more famous for his stories of Alice.

CARVER, GEORGE WASHINGTON (1864-1943) Millions of pounds of peanuts are raised in the southern states each year. Peanuts are good food, but the southern farmers raise many more of them than people eat. Much of the crop goes into salad oil, flour, cheese, shaving cream, and plastics. The southern farmers owe a great deal to George Washington Carver, the man who discovered over 300 uses for peanuts.

LEWIS CARROLL

Alice

Duchess

Tweedledee

White Queen

March Hare

Dormouse

Mad Hatter

George Washington Carver made the peanut an important Southern crop.

Carver also found many new uses for sweet potatoes and soybeans.

The baby who grew up to be the "peanut man" was born near Joplin, Mo., during the War between the States. His mother was a slave. Her master was Moses Carver. Once soldiers kidnaped the baby. To get him back his master traded a race horse for him.

After the war, although he was free, the boy stayed with Moses Carver for several years. He enjoyed working in the gardens so much that he made up his mind to get through school and become a botanist.

The boy took the last name of his former master and called himself George Washington Carver. He had already finished college when Booker T. Washington heard of him. Washington was the head of Tuskegee Institute, a Negro university in Alabama. He invited Carver to come to Tuskegee. Carver worked there for the rest of his life.

Carver did much more than help farmers find new uses for their crops. Perhaps he helped them most of all by showing them how to take care of their soil. For all that he did he was given many honors.

CASPIAN SEA The Caspian Sea is really a lake. It joins no ocean. It is called a sea because its water is salty.

The Caspian is the largest lake in the world. It is much larger than all the Great Lakes put together.

Most of this big lake is in the Soviet Union. The southern end is in Iran. The famous Volga River flows into the Caspian.

In the lake there are many fish. Eggs from the sturgeon caught there supply much of the world's caviar.

To the north and east of the Caspian there is little rain. Some of the land is dry grassland, or steppeland. Some is desert. At Baku, on the lake's western edge, there is a great oil field. Many ships sail the Caspian to carry oil away from Baku to other cities in the Soviet Union.

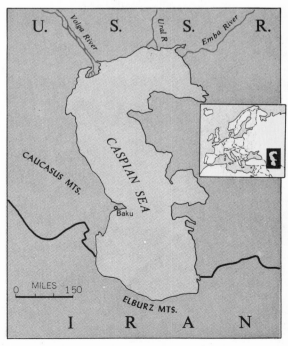

Castles were often built on hilltops.

CASTLES When we see a picture of a castle we think of fair ladies and brave knights. We think of great feasts of roasted meats in the big banquet halls, with jesters and troubadours entertaining the guests. How wonderful it must have been, it seems to us, to live in a castle!

But castles were not really very comfortable places in which to live. They were gloomy and damp and drafty. The walls inside as well as outside were cold stone. Heat came from smoky fireplaces and light from flickering torches. There was not much furniture, and there were only rushes or animal skins to cover the cold floors. A family in a small modern cottage today has far more comforts than did the noblemen who lived in the finest large castles of the Middle Ages.

But at that time there was a good reason for building castles. They were really fort-

Fires warmed the great halls.

resses. In those days there were no strong nations. Each nobleman had to protect himself and his family as well as the common people round about. These common people were mostly the serfs who worked the nobleman's land.

To help the nobleman defend his castle there were vassals. Vassals served as soldiers for the nobleman in return for land he gave them.

Castles were often built on high hills overlooking the country round about. The hills made the castles hard to attack. If a castle was built on level land, it was surrounded by a moat—a deep, wide ditch filled with water. Often the water was stagnant. Drawbridges were built across the

Knights rode out garbed for battle.

moat. These bridges could be raised in case of attack.

The outside walls of a castle were high and thick. There were towers spaced along the walls. In each tower there were several openings large enough to shoot arrows through if enemies appeared.

Inside these outer walls there were usually other walls surrounding the main courtyard. The courtyard, as a rule, had several buildings in it. Besides the living quarters of the nobleman and his family, there were stables, storehouses, and kitchens. Often there was a small chapel, too. There was also a tall tower called the "keep." This was the safest part of the castle. Prisoners were kept in the keep or

Drawbridge

Outer Gatehouse

Inner Gatehouse

Stable

Outer Ward

Battlement

Moat

in dungeons down below. Secret passages were also a part of almost every castle.

Near each castle there was a village of crude wooden huts. The common people who depended on the nobleman for protection lived there. When there was danger of attack by some warring lord, the villagers took refuge inside the castle walls.

A castle could easily be destroyed with the weapons we have today. But the walls made it quite safe in the days of spears and bows and arrows.

Many famous castles look down on the Rhine and the Danube rivers. There are many scattered over the British Isles. After kings became strong they built bigger and grander castles. Windsor Castle, begun by William the Conqueror nearly 900 years ago, is still one of the royal homes of the kings and queens of England.

Ghosts are supposed to walk the halls of many castles. There are few castles about which there is not some story of a murder that happened in the past.

The medieval castles that are left are, of course, all hundreds of years old. Some of them are in ruins. Some of them are museums. Others are still being lived in. But they all stand for a way of living that people have outgrown. (See KNIGHTHOOD; MIDDLE AGES.)

Castle defenders hurled objects down on attackers.

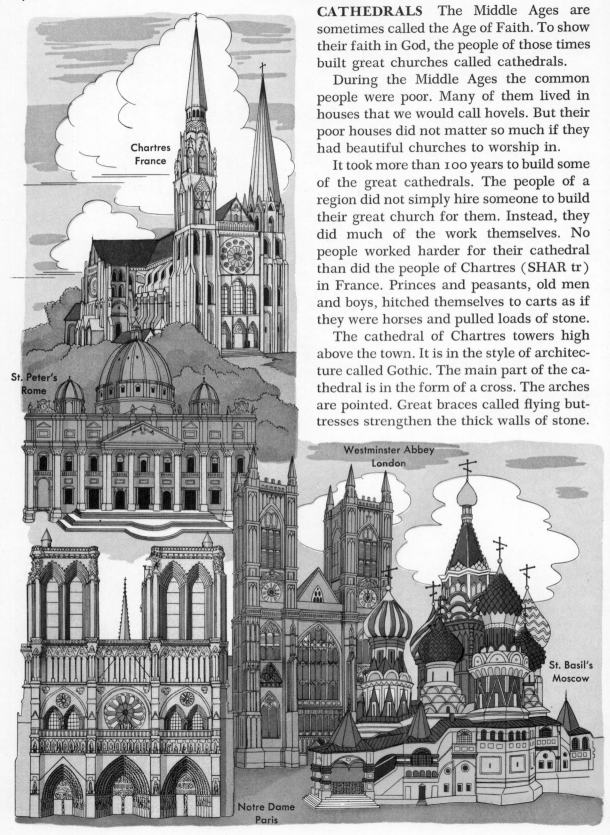

Chartres
France

St. Peter's
Rome

Notre Dame
Paris

Westminster Abbey
London

St. Basil's
Moscow

CATHEDRALS

CATHEDRALS The Middle Ages are sometimes called the Age of Faith. To show their faith in God, the people of those times built great churches called cathedrals.

During the Middle Ages the common people were poor. Many of them lived in houses that we would call hovels. But their poor houses did not matter so much if they had beautiful churches to worship in.

It took more than 100 years to build some of the great cathedrals. The people of a region did not simply hire someone to build their great church for them. Instead, they did much of the work themselves. No people worked harder for their cathedral than did the people of Chartres (SHAR tr) in France. Princes and peasants, old men and boys, hitched themselves to carts as if they were horses and pulled loads of stone.

The cathedral of Chartres towers high above the town. It is in the style of architecture called Gothic. The main part of the cathedral is in the form of a cross. The arches are pointed. Great braces called flying buttresses strengthen the thick walls of stone.

Magnificent stained glass windows and hundreds of figures carved from stone help make the cathedral beautiful. The high-arched ceiling and the soft light coming through the stained glass windows make the inside of the cathedral awe-inspiring and give an air of mystery.

A cathedral of the Middle Ages was the center of the life of the town. The people for miles around gathered there to worship. They came for Christmas and other special celebrations. At times there were plays that told stories of the lives of saints.

Today building cathedrals does not play as important a part in the lives of most people as it did in Europe in the Middle Ages. But cathedral-building did not stop with the coming of modern times. One of the well-known modern cathedrals is St. Patrick's Cathedral in the city of New York.

Many of the finest cathedrals, both medieval and modern, are Gothic like the cathedral of Chartres. But, as the pictures show, others are built in other styles. (See ARCHITECTURE; STAINED GLASS.)

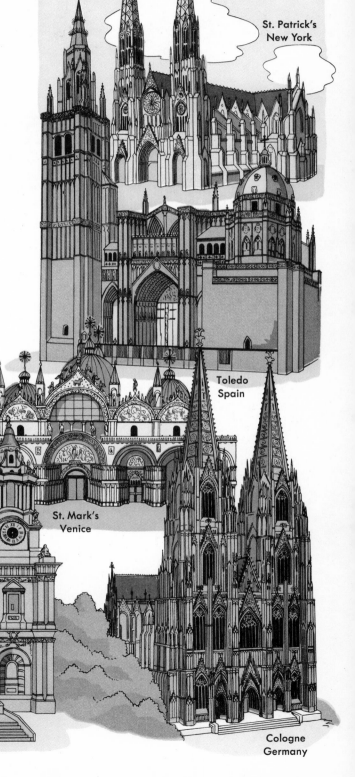

St. Patrick's New York

Toledo Spain

St. Paul's London

St. Mark's Venice

Cologne Germany

CAT FAMILY TREE

Mountain Lion

Jaguar

Lion

Jaguarundi

Cheetah

Sabertooth   Lynx

CATS The house cat and its cousins make up a large mammal family. The lion, tiger, leopard, and jaguar are all members of the cat family. So are the ocelot, cheetah, and many others besides.

The cat family is an old one. Many kinds of cats have long since disappeared. The sabertooth, which was common in the great Ice Age, is one of them.

The cats of today vary greatly in size. But whether they are big like the lion or small like the house cat, all cats are alike in a number of ways.

All of them have cushioned feet. The cushions help them move silently. Cats have sharp claws, but all except the cheetah can pull in their claws when they do not need to use them.

All cats are meat eaters. Their sharp claws help them catch other animals. They have long, sharp teeth good for tearing meat. They have rough tongues, too, that can file bits of meat from bones. Cats do most of their hunting at night. Usually they move slowly and silently up to their prey and pounce on it. But some cats have special tricks. An ocelot may hide in a tree until an animal passes by and then jump down on the animal. A jaguar may lie on a low branch over a stream and reach down into the water to catch fish.

All cats have long whiskers. The whiskers serve as feelers. Cats' eyes are usually yellow with long, slitlike pupils. At night the pupils open up wide, so that cats can see well in dim light. Cats' ears are so good that hunters find it almost impossible to slip up on any member of the cat family without being heard.

The big cats—lions, tigers, and leopards —are found chiefly in warm regions. There are smaller cats almost everywhere except in the regions near the poles.

The house cat was not tamed nearly so soon as the dog or the pig. But, even so, it was tamed long ago. Probably it was first tamed in Egypt. At least, we know that more than 4,000 years ago the Egyptians kept tame cats. They even worshiped them.

Today if we want a pet cat we have several kinds to choose from. Some are long-haired; some are short-haired.

The long-haired cats are Persians. They come in many colors: black, white, cream, buff, blue-cream, and smoke. Then, too, there are some with stripes or spots.

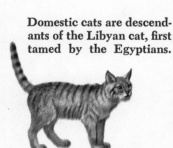

Domestic cats are descendants of the Libyan cat, first tamed by the Egyptians.

The Egyptians embalmed cats and buried them in temples.

Persians

Domestic Short-hair

Siamese

The Siamese is one of the aristocrats of the short-haired cats. Siamese cats are white when they are kittens. But they become tan with brown faces, feet, ears, and tails when they grow up. The eyes of Siamese cats are blue instead of the usual yellow. Burmese and Abyssinian cats are much like Siamese.

Another of the short-hairs is the Manx. Manx cats have no tails. Our common short-haired cats are sometimes called "alley cats." The right name is "domestic short-hairs." Many of them are tabby cats; they have wavy stripes. Other short-haired cats are white, black, buff, or blue-gray. The blue-gray cats are called Maltese. Some "alley cats" have markings of several colors.

Cats are fun to keep as pets. No baby animals are more playful than kittens. Cats are easy to care for. They can look after themselves better than most pets.

Farmers like to have cats about their barns because the cats catch many mice and rats. Unfortunately, they also catch birds. People who like birds usually are not fond of cats.

A mother cat takes good care of her kittens. When they are first born they are quite helpless. Their eyes are closed. The mother cat feeds her babies with milk from her own body, as all mammal mothers do. She keeps them clean by using her rough tongue as a washcloth. She watches to see that they do not stray away. If a mother cat has to move her kittens, she carries them with her mouth by the loose skin at the backs of their necks.

There are many wrong ideas about cats. One of them is that a cat has nine lives. Of course it has only one. Another foolish idea is that a black cat brings bad luck to a person by crossing his path. (See LION; MAMMALS; PETS; TIGER.)

Much of the grazing land of the West is still open range.

CATTLE People have tamed many kinds of animals. None of them have been more useful than the cow. Today in the United States alone there are about a hundred million cattle. There are millions more in other parts of the world.

The cow was tamed a very long time ago. Probably the big wild ox called the aurochs was the ancestor of most of our cattle. Our cave man ancestors in Europe hunted the aurochs. This wild ox is extinct.

Ever since the prehistoric times when people first learned to tame animals and to raise plants for food, cattle have not only furnished meat and milk but have also served as work animals. In American pioneer days teams of cattle, called oxen, were more common than teams of horses. In many lands cattle are still beasts of burden.

Cattle have long been used as work animals.

In the thousands of years since people began raising cattle, they have developed many breeds. Some of these breeds are especially good for milk; they are good dairy cattle. Others are especially good for beef. Still others are all-purpose breeds. They are fairly good for both beef and milk.

Four of the breeds in the picture at the bottom of the next page are common dairy breeds. They are the Jersey, Guernsey, Holstein, and Brown Swiss. The Brown Swiss is the oldest breed we know about. Its history can be traced back to the Swiss Lake Dwellers. The Jersey and the Guernsey originated in the British Isles. Early Dutch settlers in America developed the Holstein from cattle brought from the Netherlands. The Holstein is the most popular dairy cow. It gives a great deal of milk. The Jersey gives less milk than the Holstein, but the milk is much richer.

The Hereford is a beef breed common in the United States. By comparing the Hereford with the Texas longhorn one can see the progress breeders have made. Texas longhorns roamed the range in the days of Buffalo Bill. They were descendants of cattle brought to the New World by the Spanish explorers.

The beef breeds of today came mostly from England and Scotland. The Hereford originated in England. So did the Shorthorn, another good beef breed. Still another, the black Angus, came from Scotland.

One type of Shorthorn is called the Milking Shorthorn. It is good for both meat and milk. The Red Polled is another all-purpose breed. It came from England.

In some parts of the world the cattle are quite different from those we are used to seeing. The Brahman looks strange to us, but in India it is common. These Indian humped cattle are sometimes called "sacred cattle." The Hindus use them only for work and for milk, never for food. The cattle raised in South Africa have humps, too. They are called Afrikanders.

The humped cattle of Africa and India can stand hot weather better than most common breeds of cattle can. Some breeders are crossing humped cattle with our breeds to try to get cattle that will do well in the hot, humid climate of the deep South.

Young cattle are called calves. The meat of calves is sold as veal. The skin of calves is made into very fine leather. Many of our shoes are made of calfskin. Cowhide also makes good leather.

A cow pasture in the middle of a summer day is usually a peaceful looking place.

Texas longhorns once ran wild.

Most of the cows are likely to be lying in the shade chewing their cuds. All cattle are cud-chewers. As they walk about in a pasture they bite off grass and swallow it without chewing it much. Later, when the cows are resting, this grass comes up into their mouths again and the cows chew it thoroughly. The balls of grass are the cuds.

Cud-chewing must have begun back in the days when all plant-eating animals had to eat fast and be ready to run for their lives when a meat-eating animal came near. Our cattle in their fine barns and fenced-in pastures have very different lives from those of their wild ancestors. (See ANIMAL BREEDING; BISON; DAIRYING; DOMESTICATED ANIMALS; HOOFED ANIMALS; HYBRIDS; MEAT AND MEAT-PACKING; MILK; ZEBU.)

Holstein

Swiss

Hereford

Jersey

Guernsey

Brahman

People sought shelter during the Ice Age.

CAVE MEN In southern France and northern Spain there are many caves. During the last part of the great Ice Age many of these caves were used as homes by the people who lived in Europe in those days. These people we now call the cave men.

Several times during the Ice Age great sheets of ice pushed down from the north and then melted back. Scientists have discovered that there were people in Europe some 100,000 years ago, before the last great push of ice from the north. These people left many signs behind them.

As the ice pushed southward the climate grew colder and colder. The people had been living in the open. Perhaps they had simple shelters made of tree branches. But because of the cold they needed better shelters. They moved into the caves.

To live in the caves themselves they had to drive out giant cave bears and many other animals. They were able to drive out these animals partly because they knew how to make fire. A flaming torch was a very good weapon against an animal. Besides, they had weapons made of stone—stone axes and stone knives.

The early cave men had only one way of getting food—hunting. When they killed an animal, they brought it to the cave and cooked it. The bones they threw aside. When there were too many ashes around the fire, they pushed these aside, too, and covered up the bones. Once in a while a cave man lost one of his stone tools in the ashes. Scientists have been able to find out a great deal about the cave men by digging through the ashes left in the caves.

After the early cave men had lived in the caves for thousands of years, the ice began to melt back. Then a new people pushed into Europe from the south.

These later cave men were tall and strong. They were much more like the people of today. They had good brains—at least we can guess that they had from the size and shape of their skulls. They made some weapons of bone, but they still made most of their weapons of stone. They, too, got their food by hunting. They had not learned to tame any animals or grow plants. They did not make pottery. Their only clothing was made from animal skins.

But in one way they were far ahead of the early cave men. They drew excellent colored pictures of animals on the walls of

Women tanned animal hides.

Men defended themselves from wild animals.

Cave men made tools of stone.

Giant bears had to be forced from their caves before people could move in.

their caves. Many of the pictures show animals which have not been in the region for a very long time. Among these animals are mammoths and bison.

To get to some of the rooms where the pictures are, one has to crawl through narrow passageways. Many of the pictures are on the ceilings.

The caves are so dark that the cave men must have had lights of some kind. Perhaps they burned dry moss or sticks.

These cave men also made models of animals. Some of them are so good that an artist of today would be proud to have made them. The handles of many bone tools were carved into animal shapes.

The time in which the cave men lived is often called the Old Stone Age. It is named from the crude stone weapons the cave men used. The Old Stone Age in Europe ended more than 8,000 years ago.

With the retreat of the ice, people could work out better ways of living. Other people moved into Europe and mingled with the cave dwellers. Better tools were developed, and homes more comfortable than caves were built. The New Stone Age began. (See ARCHEOLOGY; ICE AGE.)

Language grew slowly, word by word.

Some cave men painted very well.

Carlsbad Caverns are probably the world's largest.

CAVERNS In 1901 a cowboy in New Mexico was puzzled by a huge swarm of bats he saw at dusk. Every evening the bats rose from a certain spot in the hills. The cowboy, Jim White, decided to explore the spot. When he did, he discovered the entrance to a system of caverns which was later named the Carlsbad Caverns. This system of caverns is perhaps the largest in the world. It is so big that parts of it have not yet been explored.

Caverns are caves made by ground water. The water dissolves rock deep underground. Most caverns are in limestone.

A limestone cavern starts with a crack in a layer of limestone. Water gets into this crack, dissolves some of the rock, and makes the crack wider. Year by year the crack grows until it has widened out into a room. If there are other cracks near by, they may become rooms too. In time some of the walls between rooms may be dissolved. If the cavern is deep enough below the surface of the ground, the layers of rock on top make a strong roof.

At first a cavern is filled with water. But it is not a real cavern until the water drains away, at least from the upper part.

Some limestone caverns are underground fairylands. After ground water has made a cavern and drained out, beautiful icicles and curtains of stone in strange and varied patterns may form.

The stone icicles are made by water dripping from the roof of the cavern. The water carries a load of minerals it has dissolved from rocks it has traveled through. As it drips, some of the water evaporates, leaving behind the minerals it was carrying. A tiny stone icicle begins to form. More water runs down the icicle. Some of it evaporates before it falls to the floor. The icicle grows larger.

The water dripping from an icicle keeps hitting the same spot on the floor. An upside down icicle begins to form there. At last the two may grow together to form a pillar of stone.

A stone icicle hanging from the ceiling of a cave is called a stalactite (sta LAK tite). One that grows up from the floor is a stalagmite (sta LAG mite). There is an easy way to remember which is which. "Stalactite" has a *c* in it. Stalactites hang from the ceiling.

Sometimes the water drips from a long crack in the ceiling. Then a thin rock curtain is formed. Sometimes water flows down over a wall. It may form a "frozen waterfall" of stone. Sometimes the minerals form flowerlike crystals on the walls. It is hard for anyone who has never seen a big cavern to imagine how beautiful and full of surprises one can be.

Bats leave their caverns at dusk to find food.

Colorful rock formations make a cavern an underground fairyland.

There are many caverns in different parts of the world. One of the most famous is Mammoth Cave, in Kentucky.

To see all the rooms and passages in Mammoth Cave a person would have to travel nearly 200 miles. Some of the walls in this cavern are as high as a five-story building. There are many streams and pools in it. Visitors can travel in boats on some of the streams.

The temperature in Mammoth Cave stays the same night and day, summer and winter. It is 54°F. In the waters of Mammoth Cave there are both fish and crayfish. But they are blind. Since caverns are pitch dark, these fish and crayfish would not be able to see even if they had good eyes.

To the people of today caverns are interesting places to visit. They were much more important to the people of long ago. Caverns were homes for our cave-man ancestors. (See CAVE MEN.)

Exploring a cavern requires great care.

One-celled Animals, or Protozoa.

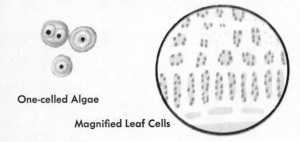

One-celled Algae

Magnified Leaf Cells

CELL All living things—lions, butterflies, grass, elm trees, dogs, people, and everything else alive—are built of cells. There are millions of cells in the bodies of most plants and animals. Some plants and animals, however, are made up of just one cell.

Not all cells are the same shape or size. Some, such as red blood cells, are disk-shaped while others, such as muscle cells, are long and narrow. Nerve cells have very irregular shapes. Some plant cells are brick-shaped while others are round. There are many other shapes of both plant and animal cells, too. Most cells are far, far too small to be seen without a microscope. Some are just barely large enough to be seen with the naked eye. And some, because of the food stored in them, are rather large. The yolk of a newly-formed hen's egg, for instance, is a cell.

Different kinds of cells do different kinds of work. Certain animal cells carry messages. Others carry oxygen. Some fight diseases. Still others make the animal move. Some plant cells take in water. Some manufacture food, and so on.

In some ways, however, all cells are alike. They all have a wall around them and a jellylike substance inside. This jellylike substance is called protoplasm. Most cells have in them a tiny, round body of thickened protoplasm. It is called the nucleus. The nucleus is the "ruler" of the cell. It governs the life of the cell and makes the cell do the work it is supposed to do.

Without protoplasm, cells would not be alive. In turn, nothing is alive that is not made of cells, for only cells have protoplasm. (See AMEBA; BLOOD; MICROSCOPE; PROTOZOA.)

CENSUS This encyclopedia tells about many countries. In each case it tells how many people live there. No one would know these figures if countries did not count their people from time to time. Counting the people of a place is called "taking a census."

In the United States a census is taken every ten years—in every year that ends in zero. Taking a census is not easy. The government finds out many things besides the number of people. It finds out, among other things, what work people do, how old they are, what kinds of homes they live in, and whether they have radios, telephones, and television sets.

The United States might take a census more often if it were not so expensive. Many workers must be hired to go from door to door to ask questions. Many other workers are needed to put together the reports that come in. More than 130,000 workers took part in the 1950 census.

Not all countries take a census in the same year. For this reason a date is sometimes given after a population figure. It tells the date of the census. In between census years many places estimate their population. Some states of the United States take censuses of their own in between national censuses.

The first United States census was taken in 1790. But the idea of a census was not at all new then. Census-taking goes back to

CENTIPEDE The word "centipede" comes from two Latin words meaning "hundred legs." Some centipedes have more than a hundred legs. They may have over 300! Some have fewer. The common house centipede has only 30.

The body of a centipede is divided into rings, or segments. On its head a centipede has a pair of feelers. On the first segment back of its head it has two poison claws which it uses to catch tiny animals for food. On every other segment back to the last two it has two legs for walking. Centipedes do not all have the same number of legs because they do not all have the same number of segments.

In India there is a kind of centipede that grows to be a foot long. But most centipedes are much shorter. The house centipede is about an inch long. Some of its legs are longer than its body. They are so long and delicate that it is almost impossible to catch a house centipede without breaking off some of its legs.

Most centipedes live under logs or stones, where it is dark and damp. House centipedes usually live in damp basements.

Many people are afraid of centipedes, but most of them do not harm people. Only the large centipedes of the tropics are dangerous to humans.

Baby centipedes hatch from eggs. The eggs are usually laid in the ground.

OFFICIAL U.S. CENSUS FIGURES

Year	Population
1790*	3,929,214
1800	5,308,483
1850	23,191,876
1900	75,994,575
1950	151,132,000
1960#	179,358,000

*—First U.S. Census
#—Estimated population

ancient times. It is as old as collecting taxes and building an army. In fact, it is closely tied up with taxes and armies. Rulers of long ago counted their people chiefly to find out how much tax money they could get and how many men they would be able to call to fight.

Today a population count has many other purposes. It gives a picture of what is happening in a country. It shows such things as which parts of the country are growing fastest and where new schools and roads are needed.

There are other kinds of censuses besides population counts. They give figures about such things as manufacturing, mining, and farming. All censuses help governments plan for the present and the future. (See TAXES.)

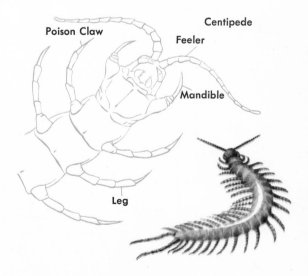

Poison Claw · Centipede · Feeler · Mandible · Leg

Sailfish

Mayan Stela

Volcanoes

Bananas

COFFEE

Cotton

Chicle

M E X I C O

BR. HONDURAS

Belize

GULF OF HONDURAS

G U A T E M A L A

Cobán

Pto. Barrios

Zacapa

Totonicapán

Comalapa

Chimaltenango

Quezaltenango

Guatemala

Antigua

Mazatenango

Escuintla

Tela

Puerto Cortés

San Pedro Sula

Progresso

La Ceiba

Santa Rosa de Copán

H O N D U R A S

Tegucigalpa

Boundary claimed by Nicaragua

Patuca River

Coco River

Santa Ana

Ahuachapán

Suchitoto

Sonsonate

Neuva San Salvador

San Vicente

San Salvador

Zacatecoluca

San Miguel

EL SALVADOR

Choluteca

Matagalpa

Chinandega

N I C A R A G U A

León

Lake Managua

Managua

Masaya

Granada

Diriamba

Jinotepe

Rivas

Lake Nicaragua

San Juan River

MOSQUITO COAST

Bluefields

P A C I F I C

O C E A N

C O S T A

Puntarenas

Alajuela

Hered

San José

Cart

R I C A

Guatemala

Honduras

Nicaragua

Panama

British Honduras

Costa Rica

FLAGS OF CENTRAL AMERICA

Symbol	Meaning
S	Silver
G	Gold
	Textiles
	Fish
	Lumbering
	Cacao
S	Sugar
	Coffee
	Rice
	Shipping
	Fibers
B	Bananas

ELEVATION
Feet
Over 10000
5000-10000
2000-5000
1000-2000
0 -1000

Total population........10,679,920
Area (square miles).......208,685

0   MILES   100

CENTRAL AMERICA The long neck of land that reaches from Mexico to South America is called Central America. It is really a part of North America.

Central America is not as large as Texas, but it is divided up into six independent countries and one colony. The countries are Honduras, Nicaragua, Guatemala, Panama, Costa Rica, and El Salvador. The colony is British Honduras. There is also the Canal Zone, a strip of land ten miles wide which is a part of the United States. The Panama Canal goes through it.

On a map it looks as if Central America would be a good bridge from Mexico and the United States to South America. But it is not. Its mountains make traveling there hard. So do its steamy forests. The mountains and forests also help explain why Central America is broken up into several separate countries.

Most of the people of Central America are Indian or part Indian. The Indian houses are usually small huts, many with only one room. The walls and floors are of mud. But the huts may be gay with pictures on the walls and with bright-colored pots and pans. For cooking there is a small stove in the middle of the room or out of doors. On the stoves the women bake tortillas. Tortillas are flat cakes made of cornmeal. They serve as bread. Many a meal in Central America is made up of tortillas, beans, coffee, and plantains. Plantains are a kind of banana.

The land along the coast of the Caribbean Sea is low. So is the land along the Pacific. All the rest is high. Most of the people live in the highlands. The lowlands are so hot and wet that they are not pleasant places to live.

These low, wet lands, however, are just right for growing bananas. There are so many banana plantations there that the six countries of Central America are sometimes called the "banana republics."

The eastern lowlands that have not been cleared for banana plantations are covered with dense forests. Workers cut lumber and gather chicle in these forests. Chicle is used

Market day is exciting in Central America.

in chewing gum. Mahogany is one of the kinds of wood they cut. It is an excellent wood for furniture because of its strength and beauty. Along the Pacific, sugar cane shares the lowlands with bananas. In many of the lowland areas, cacao, too, is raised.

Coffee and corn are two big crops of the highlands. The Indians there were raising corn long before white people ever saw or heard of corn. The people of Central America use most of the corn they raise, but they ship much coffee to other lands. Beef cattle are raised in the highlands, too, and some beef is being exported.

Central America has stores of minerals. So far, however, many are not mined.

The climate in many places in the highlands is very pleasant. Some of these places are good spots for a winter vacation. Guatemala City, Central America's largest city, is one of the pleasant vacation spots. Many tourists go there.

Market day brings whole families to Guatemala City from the countryside round about. Wearing gay costumes, people come from as far as 10 or 15 miles away to sell things that they have raised. They bring beans, corn, and other vegetables. They bring chickens and eggs, too. Some families have oxcarts to ride in. Some have mules with saddlebags. But some of them have to walk all the way. The father may carry a big sack of corn and beans on his back. The mother may carry eggs or vegetables in a basket on her head. Even the children must do their share. Perhaps each child carries a live chicken, a bag of beans, or a few ears of corn.

People go to Guatemala to see such colorful scenes as market day. They go also for the pleasant climate and to visit the ruins left behind by the Mayas. The Mayas were Indians who had a great empire long before the days of Columbus.

Indians search for mahogany and chicle in the forests.

Unfortunately there have been many wars in Central America. Most of the fighting has not been between country and country. It has been between different groups of people inside the various countries. This fighting has kept the people from making as much progress as they might have made. (See BALBOA; BANANAS; MAYAS; PANAMA CANAL; SUGAR.)

Towns of Central America look like Spanish towns.

Why doesn't the stone fall down?

CENTRIFUGAL FORCE

CENTRIFUGAL FORCE When a muddy car wheel spins around, it flings off some of the mud that is on it. The force that makes the mud fly off is called centrifugal force. "Centrifugal" comes from Latin words which mean "running away from the center."

The boy in the picture is experimenting with centrifugal force. He is whirling a stone tied to a string. Suppose instead he were whirling a bucket full of water around him. The water would not come out. It would be thrown against the bottom of the bucket by centrifugal force. The bucket might be upside down part of the time, and still the water would stay in.

Anyone who has watched the hammer-throw at a track meet has seen centrifugal force at work. The hammer is a weight on the end of a slender rod. The faster it is whirled, the harder centrifugal force pulls it outward. At last the thrower lets go, and the hammer sails away.

Dairy farmers find centrifugal force very helpful in separating cream from milk. In a cream separator the milk is whirled around very fast. Cream is rather light. It stays near the center. The heavier part of the milk is whirled to the outside and drained away.

It is a good thing that another force called gravity is always pulling us. If it weren't, centrifugal force would throw us off into space as the earth whirls around! (See GRAVITY.)

CENTURY PLANT The century plant grows in the deserts of Mexico and south-western United States. Like many desert plants, it has big thick leaves.

When the century plant is ready to bloom, it sends up a huge flower stalk. The stalk may grow to be a foot across at the base and 20 feet tall. There are hundreds of flowers on the stalk. As soon as these flowers wither, the plant dies. A century plant never blooms more than once.

The real name of the century plant is agave (a GAY vee). It got the name "century plant" from the old idea that it had to grow for a hundred years—a century—to bloom. Actually a century plant blooms when it has stored up enough food and water in its leaves to produce the big flower stalk. In the warm Mexican deserts a century plant may bloom when it is only ten years old. But in hothouses in cool lands it may really need 100 years to store up enough food and water for its single great bouquet of flowers.

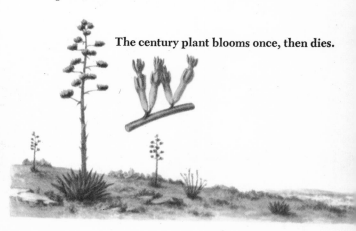

The century plant blooms once, then dies.

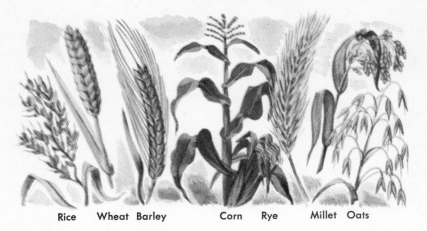

Rice　Wheat Barley　　Corn　Rye　　Millet Oats

CEREALS The grass family is the most important of all plant families. In it are wheat, corn, rice, rye, oats, barley, and millet. These grains make up a very large part of the world's food. Often they are called cereals. This name comes from Ceres, the name of the ancient Roman goddess of vegetation.

The word "cereal" is also used for breakfast foods made from these grains. Oatmeal is one of the common breakfast cereals. Oatmeal and many other cereals must be cooked before they are eaten. They are usually eaten hot. Cornflakes and similar breakfast cereals come ready-to-eat. They are usually eaten cold.

The grain used for breakfast cereals may be crushed, dried, roasted, puffed up by steam, or rolled into thin flakes. Salt, sugar, molasses, or raisins may be added.

Cereals are important in our diets. Food experts tell us that we should have cereal every day. From grains we get some food materials that we cannot get easily in other ways. These materials are certain minerals and vitamins. Many of these minerals and vitamins are in the outside covering of the grain. This outside covering is often thrown away when breakfast cereals are manufactured. We get more of these materials if the whole grain is used. (See CORN; GRASSES; RICE; WHEAT.)

Rice is raised in China in terraced fields that are flooded with water.

Giant machines which cut the wheat, thresh it, and bundle the straw are common on large farms in midwestern United States. These machines are called combines.

THE GOLDEN BOOK ENCYCLOPEDIA

CONTAINS THE FOLLOWING VOLUMES

I	Aardvark to Army	IX	Labor Day to Matches
II	Arthur to Blood	X	Mathematics to Natural Gas
III	Boats to Cereals	XI	Navy to Parasites
IV	Chalk to Czechoslovakia	XII	Paricutin to Quicksand
V	Daguerreotype to Epiphyte	XIII	Rabbits to Signaling
VI	Erosion to Geyers	XIV	Silk to Textiles
VII	Ghosts to House Plants	XV	Thailand to Volcanoes
VIII	Hudson to Korea	XVI	Wales to Zoos—Index

CONTRIBUTING ARTISTS

Dot and Sy Barlowe • Cornelius De Witt • E. Joseph Dreany • Bruno Frost
James Gordon Irving • Beth and Joe Krush • Harry Lazarus • Andre LeBlanc
H. Charles McBarron • Denny McMains • Harry McNaught
Ray Perlman • John Polgreen • Evelyn Urbanowich

Pauline Batchelder Adams • George Avison • Barry Bart • Ernie Barth • Charles Bellow
Eric Bender • Juanita Bennett • Merrit Berger • Robert D. Bezucha • William Bolin
Thelma Bowie • Matilda Breuer • S. Syd Brown • Peter Buchard • Louise Fulton Bush
Jim Caraway • Nino Carbe • Sam Citron • Gordon Clifton • Mel Crawford • Robert Doremus
Harry Daugherty • Rachel Taft Dixon • Olive Earle • Sydney F. Fletcher • F. Beaumont Fox
Rudolf Freund • Tibor Gergely • Douglas Gorsline • Hamilton Greene • Gerald Gregg
Marjorie Hartwell • Hans H. Helweg • Janice Holland • W. Ben Hunt
Arch and Miriam Hurford • Harper Johnson • Norman Jonsson • Matthew Kalmenoff
Janet Robson Kennedy • Paul Kinnear • Olga Kucera • Walter Kumme • John Leone
Kenneth E. Lowman • John Alan Maxwell • Jean McCammack • Shane Miller • Stina Nagel
Elizabeth Newhall • Gregory Orloff • Raymond Pease • Alice and Martin Provensen
Jerry Robinson • Feodor Rojankovsky • Roki • Mary Royt • Arnold W. Ryan
Arthur Sanford • Sam Savitts • William Sayles • Al Schmidt • Edwin Schmidt
Frederick E. Seyfarth • Robert Sherman • George Solonewitsch • Lionel Stern
Norton Stewart • Valerie Swenson • Gustaf Tenggren • William Thompson • Felix Traugott
Eileen Fox Vaughn • Herschel Wartik • Robert Weisman • Garth Williams

MAPS BY

Vincent Kotschar   Jean Paul Tremblay
Carol Vinall   Frederic Lorenzen
Rudolf von Siegl   Francis Barkoczy

COVER ARTISTS

Ned Seidler • Ken Davies • Don Moss